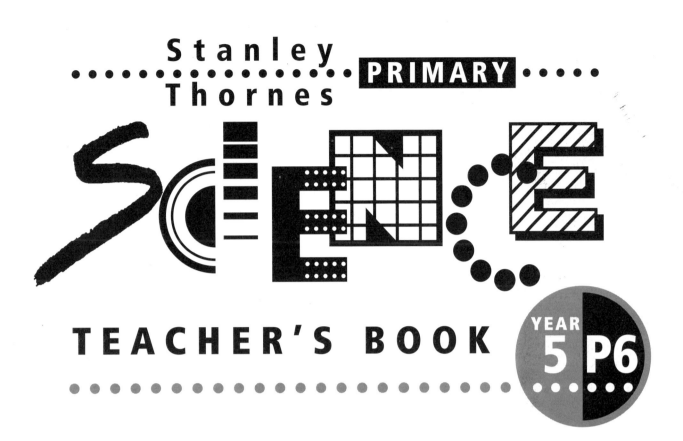

Stanley Thornes **PRIMARY**

SCIENCE

TEACHER'S BOOK

YEAR 5 P6

Wendy Clemson and David Clemson

STANLEY THORNES

First published in 1997 by

Stanley Thornes Publishers Ltd
Ellenborough House
Wellington Street
Cheltenham GL50 1YD

97 98 99 00 01/ 10 9 8 7 6 5 4 3 2 1

A catalogue record for this book is available from the British Library.

ISBN 0-7487-2964-X

Design and typesetting by DP Press, Sevenoaks, Kent

Printed and bound in Great Britain by Redwood Books, Trowbridge, Wiltshire

ACKNOWLEDGEMENTS

Teacher's Book and Resources artists: Juliette Nicholson, Philip Orchard, Clyde Pearson.

Poster illustrations are by or used with the permission of the following:

Unit 1, Lesson 9
Rocks and minerals

Rose quartz	Wayland Picture Library
Limestone	Wayland Picture Library
Granite	Wayland Picture Library
Marble	Wayland Picture Library
Slate	Wayland Picture Library
Sandstone	Wayland Picture Library
Gypsum	Topham Picturepoint
Clay	Topham Picturepoint
Haematite	GeoScience Features Picture Library

Unit 1, Lesson 11
Firework safety

Girl with sparkler	Topham Picturepoint

Unit 2, Lesson 5
Hygiene
Chris Ryley

Unit 2, Lesson 10
Ant colony
Clyde Pearson

Unit 3, Lesson 1
Magnets

Cable car	Heights of Abraham
Monorail	Alton Towers
Scrap metal magnet	Rotary Burnard
Walkman	The Science Museum/Science and Society Picture Library

Unit 4, Lesson 4
Leaf varieties

Horse chestnut	Wayland Picture Library
Yew	Klein/Hubert/Still Pictures
Alder	Klein/Hubert/Still Pictures
Ash	Wayland Picture Library
Holly	Topham Picturepoint
Beech	Ann Robinson/Topham Picturepoint
Hawthorn	Topham Picturepoint
Mountain Ash	Topham Picturepoint
Scots pine	Topham Picturepoint
Lime	Mark Antman/Topham Picturepoint
Oak	Wayland Picture Library

Unit 4, Lesson 7
Litter
Clyde Pearson

Unit 5, Lesson 3
Shadows
Chris Ryley

Unit 5, Lesson 8
The night sky
Philip Orchard

Unit 5, Lesson 10
The Moon

First quarter Moon	Wayland Picture Library
Gibbous Moon	Robin Scagell/Galaxy
Last quarter Moon	Galaxy Picture Library
Full Moon from Apollo 11 spacecraft	NASA/Genesis Space Photo Library
Moon surface view (far side)	NASA
Part of far side of the Moon	NASA/Galaxy

Contents

Foreword

Our aim in writing Stanley Thornes Primary Science is to give teachers the means of making available to children some of the important ideas in science and being a scientist. We have been asked to make Stanley Thornes Primary Science cover the National Curriculum, and 5–14 Guidelines in Scotland, because that is what teachers are now obliged to do. Though time for teachers and space for authors is short, we have attempted to do more than that. One of the authors had a physics teacher who referred to 'common sense' as the kind that is called common but is not always so. We all of us talk about 'general knowledge' which often is not so either. Using Stanley Thornes Primary Science as a start we hope that teachers will be able to help children not only learn some very specific scientific facts and ways of working, but also acquire 'the sense of science' that should be 'common', and an abundance of 'knowledge of science' that should be 'general'. We should like children to leave the primary school with some ideas about what it means to be a natural historian, and be able to describe and in some cases explain a variety of phenomena. In addition we should like children to gain the conviction that science is accessible, useful and entertaining.

Wendy Clemson
David Clemson

Introduction

Stanley Thornes Primary Science is a course for the complete primary age range. In England and Wales the Schools Curriculum and Assessment Authority recommends that children should experience at least 54 hours of science in a school year, at Key Stage 1, and at least 72 hours at Key Stage 2. In Scotland children are expected to spend 25% of their time on Environmental Studies, including science. This course provides sufficient work to meet those recommendations.

For each year there are the following components:

- One Teacher's Book
- One photocopiable Resource file
- 12 Posters

THE ORGANISATION

In Years 3–6/P4–P7 the year's work is arranged in six units of study, each having 12 one-hour lessons. It is anticipated that a unit will be covered in half a term.

There is a common layout for all the units. At the beginning is a general introduction. Special resources and advance planning requirements for the unit are listed, along with the kinds of topics to seek out among library and multimedia sources. This is followed by a unit map which lists all the learning intentions for the forthcoming lessons.

In Year 5/P6 the units are as follows:

Unit 1:   Solids, liquids and gases
Unit 2:   Body works
Unit 3:   Important forces
Unit 4:   Living things in their environment
Unit 5:   Sound, light and the solar system
Unit 6:   Being a scientist

THE TEACHER'S BOOK

The lessons are laid out consistently on double page spreads, so that the book can be left open during the lesson. Each lesson is planned to accommodate whole classes of children of mixed ability.

Facsimiles of the poster and photocopiable resources needed for each lesson are reproduced here.

There are three learning intentions for every lesson. Learning intention **A** should be met by all the children. It is anticipated that most children will succeed at learning intention **b**; whilst **C** will be for some of the children.

This is a suggestion about how the children should be organised through the lesson, in order to complete the activities.

'Watchpoints' offer advice on safety points and unexpected outcomes.

Essential vocabulary is listed.

The activities spell out exactly what the children are required to do to meet each of the learning intentions.

The expected results are set out to match the activities **A**, **b** and **C** which in turn, accord with the learning intentions **A**, **b** and **C**.

UNIT 1
Solids, liquids and gases
LESSON 2
About matter

Learning intentions

A Know some of the properties of solids, liquids and gases.

b Know about ways we use solids, liquids and gases.

C Investigate the use of solids, liquids and gases in brakes.

Vocabulary

Gas, liquid, pour, shape, solid, volume

Lesson pattern

Whole class, Help sheet, work with a partner and Workbook page, Extend sheet

RESOURCES AND SETTING UP

A Poster 1.2. Help sheet. An empty jug, a glass jug with coloured water in it and an empty container, a balloon inflated, a second balloon and a balloon pump, a water pistol and a container of water from which the water pistol can be filled.

b Workbook page. It may be helpful to display some of the items that appear on the Workbook page.

C Extend sheet. Books or other information about the operation of bicycle, car and lorry brakes.

ACTIVITIES

INTRODUCTION

● Remind the children that everything in the universe is described by scientists in one word, 'matter'. Show the children objects around the room and point out that they are all made of matter. Show the children Poster 1.2 and use this as a stimulus for discussion.

A Show the water in the jug to the children. Pour some into a container. Compare this with a solid object like a book and say to the children that both the water and the book are matter, but how do they differ? Place the book in an empty dry jug to help with comparisons. Then show the children the balloon. Ask what is in the balloon, and then point out that this is also matter. Show the children the full water pistol. Ask what happens when the trigger is pressed. Check that all salient points emerge in discussion. Ask the children to complete the Help sheet.

b Give the children the Workbook page. In pairs they should then follow instructions and determine reasons for the uses of the materials on the Workbook page, related to the properties of solids, liquids and gases.

C The children will need to research the three kinds of brakes on the Extend sheet.

14

OUTCOMES

EXPECTED RESULTS

A The children should note that liquid pours and takes the shape of its container; air in the balloon is squeezed or compressed; water in the pistol 'resists' squeezing and is forced out of the nozzle. The three images at the bottom of the Help sheet should provide discussion points. The jelly took the shape of its container when liquid and is now 'set' in that shape; the swiss roll is solid but soft and flexible. The figurine has been made of a malleable material which retains its shape once 'fired'. During the demonstration and discussion the children should arrive at the following properties:

– solids have a fixed shape and volume, cannot be poured and are hard to squeeze.
– liquids have a fixed volume but no fixed shape, can be poured and are hard to squeeze.
– gases have neither fixed shape nor volume and can be squeezed.

b Here are some of the ideas that may appear in the children's answers:

– baby cups: lids to prevent liquid spills.
– coolbox air gap: air is a good insulator.
– air in bicycle tyres: can be compressed to form an air 'cushion'.
– metal car bodies: strong and can be shaped.

– room thermometers: liquid changes in volume in response to heat – good air temperature detector.
– metal knife blades: can be shaped to sharp edge, easy to clean.
– clay cooking pots: once fired become hard and can withstand temperature changes.
– plastic/card food packs: cheap, easy to shape and print on to.

C The important point the children should find out is that bicycle brakes use solids (the brake blocks), car brakes use a liquid and lorry brakes use air (gas) to make the connection and carry the 'message' from brake pedal to the actual brake pad or disk.

WATCHPOINTS

● Bicycle brakes are on view in Year 4/P5. Poster 1.3.

Assessment of learning outcomes

A Help sheet.

b Workbook page.

C Extend sheet.

15

There is a list of resources required, and advice on 'setting up' the lesson.

The introduction to the lesson includes details of how to 'set the scene' for what the children are learning, and carry them forward into the activities.

The spoken and written work the children have done which should contribute to an assessment of whether they have met the learning intentions is listed under 'assessment of learning outcomes'.

THE RESOURCES

The 'workbook' pages are intended for use by all the children. You may wish to staple them into workbooks. They include the following:

- Picture unit maps for the children to follow.

- Pages on which to record work done.

- Checklists for the children to complete to remind them of what they have done.

- Two-page 'tests' for the review lessons.

The 'Help' sheets offer additional information and help to some or all children and are included in lessons where appropriate. The 'Extend' sheets are for children who complete activities **A** and **b** in a lesson. They should be used to meet learning intention **C**.

Where children have recorded work on Workbook, Help and Extend sheets, these can be added to work portfolios.

Facsimiles of the resource pages and posters relevant to the lesson are reproduced on the Teacher's Book spread. Occasionally where, for example, multiple Help sheets and a poster are recommended for use during a lesson, it has only been possible to reproduce a selection of the resources, owing to space constraints. However, all resource pages are clearly labelled with the unit and lesson number.

POSTERS

The posters are used in a variety of ways. They are a teaching aid in the introduction to some lessons. They can form part of a display on the topic of the unit. The children will need them to get information in order to respond to some of the demands of the activities.

The posters in Year 5/P6 cover the following areas:

Unit 1
Solid, liquid or gas?
Rocks and minerals
Firework safety

Unit 2
Hygiene
Ant colony

Unit 3
Magnets
Aircraft

Unit 4
Leaf varieties
Litter

Unit 5
Shadows
The night sky
The Moon

. . . .

PLANNING AND PROGRESSION

Stanley Thornes Primary Science Year 5/P6 comprises six units of work each including 12 one-hour lessons. This 72-hour course has been planned to meet the national recommendations regarding the amount of time children should spend on science.

Children can, of course, spend more time on science than we suggest. If they do only the work set down in this course, we are confident that they will have met national recommendations regarding the amount of time they spend on science.

The intention is that children should gain progressively more understanding of important scientific concepts, as they move through the primary years, reaching appropriate National Curriculum levels. The levels at which the books are pitched are shown below.

It is anticipated that children will tackle one unit in each of the six half terms of the school year. The twelve lessons can be fitted into six weeks, with two one-hour lessons each week. Where a half term is longer than six weeks, this offers opportunities to:
- – do extra investigations in science,
- – re-visit concepts the children need extra work on,
- – devote time to additional science,
- – allow a week or more without science lessons (perhaps when the children are on a trip).

The units of work can be taken in any order. However, we have set them down in an order which we hope offers a variety of work for the children, maintaining interest and motivation, and takes advantage of weather conditions and seasonal changes which may affect studies of animals, plants, the Earth and light.

We have placed the unit intended to focus on Sc 1 (experimental and investigative science) at the end of the year. It is anticipated that the children will do much work in other units that gives them experience of experimental and investigative science, and that work on unit 6 will confirm and reinforce these earlier experiences.

At Key Stage 2/P4–P7 each unit comprises twelve lessons. Eleven of these contain new learning and the twelfth lesson is a review. The review lesson has in it a list of test questions on work done in the whole unit, and in addition, children can complete their own evaluation checklist. Those who finish this work are provided with an extension activity as in other lessons.

In planning the work for the children in your class, you should consult the introduction and unit map for the unit to be tackled. Look at the sections on advanced planning, and books and multimedia search in order to assemble all the additional resources and help required before starting work on the unit.

England, Wales and Northern Ireland							
Nursery & Reception / P1		Year 1 / P2	Year 2 / P3	Year 3 / P4	Year 4 / P5	Year 5 / P6	Year 6 / P7
pre Level 1 working towards Level 1 Level 1	a activities	working towards Level 1	working towards Level 2	working towards Level 2	working towards Level 3	working towards Level 4	working towards Level 5
	b activities	Level 1	Level 2	Level 2	Level 3	Level 4	Level 5
	c activities	working towards Level 2 and beyond	working towards Level 3 and beyond	working towards Level 3 and beyond	working towards Level 4 and beyond	working towards Level 5 and beyond	working towards Level 6 and beyond

Scotland							
P1		P2	P3	P4	P5	P6	P7
pre Level 1	a activities	pre Level A	working towards Level A	working towards Level A	working towards Level B	working towards Level C	working towards Level D
	b activities	working towards Level A	Level A	Level A	Level B	Level C	Level D
	c activities	Level A	working towards Level B and beyond	working towards Level B and beyond	working towards Level C and beyond	working towards Level D and beyond	working towards Level E and beyond

ASSESSMENT

Pointers to assessment opportunities are listed in each lesson. For the most part these include a scrutiny of the written work the children have done, and observation of their participation in discussion and practical work. Additionally, the test provided in the review lesson for each unit should support teacher assessments of what children have learned.

A record sheet (to be found at the end of the Resources file) can be photocopied for each child. This will provide an end-of-year summary of the work the child has done and should assist teacher assessments.

INFORMATION TECHNOLOGY

We have deliberately set out to write Stanley Thornes Primary Science without any assumptions about levels of IT resourcing in schools. We are concerned that no lesson should be inaccessible to children because the appropriate IT facilities are not on offer in their school. However, it is necessary for schools to gain access to computer power.

CD-ROMs will provide an increasingly valuable resource for scientific information. Encyclopaedias and other reference sources would be a great asset to both teachers and children in some parts of this course.

Database software is also important in studies of animals and plants. It may prove helpful to seek out databases available locally. Ask at the local information technology centre, neighbouring secondary schools, higher education institutions, and the education advisory service (if there is one), for details of databases and other information they have.

The Association for Science Education is a useful source of information for teachers and some of their publications are invaluable. *Signs, Symbols and Systematics: the ASE companion to 5–16 Science* is a very important book to have. Word roots, animal classification, circuit symbols, SI units, safety symbols; all of these are there and much more. The Association for Science Education can be contacted at College Lane, Hatfield, Hertfordshire, AL10 9AA.

ABOUT THIS UNIT

Work in this unit continues to build towards children's understanding of chemistry. The unit begins with work on the properties and uses of materials. The children learn what 'matter' is. They are then invited to identify some of the characteristics of solids, liquids and gases. They begin testing liquids with a 'home-made' indicator, and then try using litmus. This is intended as an introduction to the idea of acids and alkalis which will be met at Key stage 3. There are two lessons giving children experience in separating mixtures. There follows a discussion of change in materials, supported by work on the irreversible change involved in mixing plaster of Paris. Two lessons are devoted to the study of rocks and soils. The final lesson involves a discussion of firework safety. Children can be reminded that it is the properties in the ingredients of fireworks that make them potentially explosive. The discussion in this lesson can also be related to health and safety in school.

SPECIAL RESOURCES AND ADVANCED PLANNING

Lesson 1
A box for each work group containing material samples including, for example, wood, metal, chalk and coconut fibres is required for each work group. Household items made from a range of materials and catalogues containing pictures of household goods would also be useful. Copies of science magazines and comics would enliven the Extend activity.

Lesson 2
Two balloons, a balloon pump, a water pistol and access to a tap are essential to this lesson.

Lesson 3
Sherbet lemons (if the teacher wishes), a tin of blackberries or fresh blackberries and boiling water are required. In addition the following substances are needed: lemon juice, bath salts, washing soda, washing up liquid, orange squash, vinegar.

Lesson 4
Colourless liquids are required for testing (there are some suggestions in the lesson notes) along with litmus paper. Distilled water can be bought in car accessory shops or it may be possible to obtain it from a Secondary School science department.

Lesson 5
Iron filings, salt, sand, filter paper and funnels are required along with clamps and sands for the funnels, beakers and a jug of water.

Lesson 6
To do this experiment, each work group will require the apparatus as for lesson 5, omitting the salt.

Lesson 7
This equipment list includes two ice trays (one filled with ice cubes), a candle in a candle holder with matches, tubs which once held foodstuffs like margarine, clay or Plasticine and plaster of Paris.

Lesson 8
Sugar and salt are essential here.

Lesson 9
For each work group, a range of soil, rock and mineral samples are required, in addition to magnifiers.

Lesson 10
Samples of different top soils are required; also magnifiers, plastic gloves, minute timers and soil test kits.

Lesson 11
A fireworks box and spent firework would be useful.

BOOK AND MULTIMEDIA SEARCH

Solids, liquids and gases
Acids and alkalis
Mixtures
Salt

The Earth's composition
Igneous and sedimentary rocks
Fireworks

UNIT MAP

Lesson 1
A Investigate the appearance, hardness and flexibility of a number of materials.
b Name uses for materials based on their properties.
c Write a piece about the uses of materials for a children's magazine.

Lesson 2
A Know some of the properties of solids, liquids and gases.
b Know about ways we use solids, liquids and gases.
c Investigate the use of solids, liquids and gases in brakes.

Lesson 3
A Know that some substances are acid and some are not.
b Use a home-made indicator to detect acidity.
c Know what etching is.

Lesson 4
A Conduct litmus tests.
b Produce a neutral solution.
c Know about the pH scale.

Lesson 5
A Know what is meant by filtering a mixture.
b Separate some mixtures.
c Know of ways sieving and filtering are used in the kitchen.

Lesson 6
A Know about the use of a magnet, filtering and evaporation in separating some mixtures.
b Separate a mixture of iron filings, sand and water.
c Find out how sea salt reaches our tables.

Lesson 7
A Revise the nature of reversible and irreversible change.
b Conduct an irreversible change.
c Puzzle out some reversible and irreversible changes.

Lesson 8
A Know what a saturated solution is.
b Make a saturated solution.
c Compare saturated solutions.

Lesson 9
A Know what soils, rocks and minerals are.
b Group rocks according to characteristics.
c Know how different rocks came to be formed.

Lesson 10
A Inspect a sample of soil.
b Test soils for permeability.
c Know what a pH test does.

Lesson 11
A Know the firework safety code.
b Recognise firework dangers.
c Create firework safety slogans.

Mystery solids

Learning intentions

a Investigate the appearance, hardness and flexibility of a number of materials.

b Name uses for materials based on their properties.

c Write a piece about the uses of materials for a children's magazine.

Vocabulary

Flexibility, hardness, properties, descriptive vocabulary as required (for example, strong, brittle, elastic, hard, soft, permeable)

Lesson pattern

Whole class, group practical work and Help sheet, Workbook page, Extend sheet

RESOURCES AND SETTING UP

● A small number of sample materials for use by the teacher in the introduction (these should differ from those the children are going to use).

a Help sheet. For each work group a box containing five sample materials is required. Example materials which could be included are:

wood, metal (take away meal containers, jar lids, cans without sharp edges), chalk or limestone, coconut fibre, coal, slate, plastic 'rubber'.

The children may decide they need some equipment to conduct the tests, and so a range of likely apparatus should be available, including, for example, scissors, string, beakers, water, and items with which to tap or scratch the samples.

b Workbook page. A number of everyday household items could be put on display for the children to examine to see what materials they are made from. Catalogues of household goods would be useful.

c Extend sheet. Children's magazines containing science articles would be useful.

ACTIVITIES

INTRODUCTION

● Remind the children of the work they did in Year 3/ P4 about the characteristics of materials. Show the children some sample materials in turn (do not use those that the children will subsequently use themselves). Talk about the characteristics that can be observed. Ask the children to suggest ways of finding out other things about the materials.

a The children should, in their work groups, examine the material samples, describe their appearance and work out tests for them for hardness and flexibility. Their work should be recorded on the Help sheet.

b Using the items on display (if a display is available) and the catalogues, as support for their own ideas, the children should think of three uses for each of the materials used in **a**. The Workbook page provides a chart for their suggestions.

c The children should, with adult help, inspect some children's magazines to see how science topics are treated. They can then write a piece about materials and their uses. Some hints are available on the Extend sheet.

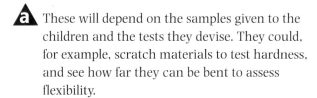

OUTCOMES

EXPECTED RESULTS

a These will depend on the samples given to the children and the tests they devise. They could, for example, scratch materials to test hardness, and see how far they can be bent to assess flexibility.

b The uses of the materials will depend on the materials themselves, and the items on display in front of the children as well as their own ideas.

c The outcomes will depend on the materials and uses the children choose.

WATCHPOINTS

● This is intended as a 'second step' lesson, following the Year 3/P4 work. It should assist children in making judgements about the connections between properties and uses of materials.

● Note that 'flexibility' as a property of metals may be difficult to detect, depending on the sample. A metal bar seems inflexible, but metal foil, metal coathangers and metal sheeting show that metals can be flexible.

⚠ Check sample materials before the lesson to ensure that none will shatter when bent.

Assessment of learning outcomes

a Help sheet.

b Workbook page.

c Extend sheet.

About matter

Learning intentions

a Know some of the properties of solids, liquids and gases.

b Know about ways we use solids, liquids and gases.

c Investigate the use of solids, liquids and gases in brakes.

Vocabulary

Gas, liquid, pour, shape, solid, volume

Lesson pattern

Whole class,
Help sheet,
work with a partner and
Workbook page,
Extend sheet

RESOURCES AND SETTING UP

a Poster 1.2, Help sheet. An empty jug, a glass jug with coloured water in it and an empty container, a balloon inflated, a second balloon and a balloon pump, a water pistol and a container of water from which the water pistol can be filled.

b Workbook page. It may be helpful to display some of the items that appear on the Workbook page.

c Extend sheet. Books or other information about the operation of bicycle, car and lorry brakes.

ACTIVITIES

INTRODUCTION

● Remind the children that everything in the universe is described by scientists in one word, 'matter'. Show the children objects around the room and point out that they are all made of matter. Show the children Poster 1.2 and use this as a stimulus for discussion.

a Show the water in the jug to the children. Pour some into a container. Compare this with a solid object like a book and say to the children that both the water and the book are matter, but how do they differ? Place the book in an empty dry jug to help with comparisons. Then show the children the balloon. Ask what is in the balloon, and then point out that this is also matter. Show the children the full water pistol. Ask what happens when the trigger is pressed. Check that all salient points emerge in discussion. Ask the children to complete the Help sheet.

b Give the children the Workbook page. In pairs they should then follow instructions and determine reasons for the uses of the materials on the Workbook page, related to the properties of solids, liquids and gases.

c The children will need to research the three kinds of brakes on the Extend sheet.

OUTCOMES

EXPECTED RESULTS

a The children should note that liquid pours and takes the shape of its container; air in the balloon is squeezed or compressed; water in the pistol 'resists' squeezing and is forced out of the nozzle. The three images at the bottom of the Help sheet should provide discussion points. The jelly took the shape of its container when liquid and is now 'set' in that shape; the swiss roll is solid but soft and flexible. The figurine has been made of a malleable material which retains its shape once 'fired'. During the demonstration and discussion the children should arrive at the following properties:

– solids have a fixed shape and volume, cannot be poured and are hard to squeeze.
– liquids have a fixed volume but no fixed shape, can be poured and are hard to squeeze.
– gases have neither fixed shape nor volume and can be squeezed.

b Here are some of the ideas that may appear in the children's answers:

– baby cups: lids to prevent liquid spills.
– coolbox air gap: air is a good insulator.
– air in bicycle tyres: can be compressed to form an air 'cushion'.
– metal car bodies: strong and can be shaped.

– room thermometers: liquid changes in volume in response to heat – good air temperature detector.
– metal knife blades: can be shaped to sharp edge, easy to clean.
– clay cooking pots: once fired become hard and can withstand temperature changes.
– plastic/card food packs: cheap, easy to shape and print on to.

c The important point the children should find out is that bicycle brakes use solids (the brake blocks), car brakes use a liquid and lorry brakes use air (gas) to make the connection and carry the 'message' from brake pedal to the actual brake pad or disk.

WATCHPOINTS

● Bicycle brakes are on view in Year 4/P5, Poster 1.3.

Assessment of learning outcomes

a Help sheet.

b Workbook page.

c Extend sheet.

Acid test

Learning intentions

a Know that some substances are acid and some are not.

b Use a home-made indicator to detect acidity.

c Know what etching is.

Vocabulary

Acid, change, indicator, test

Lesson pattern

Whole class practical work and Workbook page research and Extend sheet

RESOURCES AND SETTING UP

a Sour lemon drops or sherbet lemons, blackberries, a saucepan with boiling water in it, or a tin of blackberries and a tin opener, one mystery liquid, a jug, funnel, stand, filter paper and beakers.

b Workbook page. Each work group will need:

'mystery' liquids (enough of each for all work groups to have about 10 ml at least). These are lemon juice, bath salts or washing soda dissolved in water, washing-up liquid or clothes wash liquid in water, orange squash in water, vinegar, glass or plastic jars and beakers (at least five for each work group), jugs, overalls or aprons (for all children).

c Extend sheet. Art books showing examples of etchings and information about the etching process.

ACTIVITIES

INTRODUCTION

● Each child could be given a lemon drop or sherbet lemon. They will note that there is a sour taste when they put them on their tongues. Tell the children that this is because there is what scientists call 'acid' in the sweets. We can make test substances from plants that will tell us whether liquids are acid or not.

● Add the blackberries to the boiling water and leave to stand for a while and then pour through filter paper, or tip the tinned blackberries through the filter paper and collect the liquid juice. Point out that the blackberry juice is an 'acid test substance' or indicator. Pour a little of the liquid into a lipped beaker for each work group. Remind the children to use very little as this amount should do for all five mystery liquids.

a The children should watch the teacher demonstration in the introduction to the lesson.

b In their work groups the children should use the blackberry indicator to test the five mystery liquids. A little juice should be added to each of the liquids in turn. The children can write up the experiment on their Workbook page.

c The children should find out from the resources, what etching is and how it is carried out. Their findings can be written up on the Extend sheet.

OUTCOMES

EXPECTED RESULTS

a After the introduction the children should understand that some substances are acid.

b If the 'mystery' liquids are labelled 1 to 5 as in the resources and setting up above, the blackberry juice should turn substances 1, 3 and 5 pinkish showing they are acid.

c The children should find out that etching is done by applying a wax layer to a metal plate. A picture is then drawn through the wax surface. The metal plate is put into acid which affects the metal surface where there is no wax. Prints can then be taken from the metal plate.

WATCHPOINTS

 Warn the children that they should never try inhaling or tasting test or experimental, or any unknown, substances.

 Be careful with boiling water. Ensure the saucepan is positioned so that the children cannot knock it over.

Assessment of learning outcomes

a Participation in the introduction.

b Involvement in the experiment and Workbook page.

c Extend sheet.

The litmus test

Learning intentions

a Conduct litmus tests.

b Produce a neutral solution.

c Know about the pH scale.

Vocabulary

Acid, litmus, neutral, pH

Lesson pattern

Whole class, group work and Help sheet, whole class, group work and Workbook page, Extend sheet

---

RESOURCES AND SETTING UP

a Help sheet. The work groups will need: sample colourless liquids to test, e.g. white wine vinegar, baking soda in solution, fizzy lemonade, distilled water, litmus, beakers (two for each work group).

b Workbook page. Each work group will need:

white wine vinegar, baking soda solution, droppers, litmus.

c Extend sheet. Science books giving information about the pH scale.

ACTIVITIES

INTRODUCTION

● Remind the children of their work in lesson 3. Show them litmus paper and explain that this is an indicator made from a plant which is impregnated in paper. It turns pink when placed in acid. Invite the children to test the sample liquids.

a In their work groups the children should test the sample liquids with the litmus. They can record their work on their Help sheet.

b Call all the children together and show them what they should do in activity **b**. Tell the children that they are going to make a solution which is neither acid nor 'not acid' (i.e. 'alkali'). A solution which is neither acid nor alkali is said to be neutral. Hand out the Workbook page and go through it with the children. In their work groups the children should carry through the experiment noting how many drops of solution B it takes to make solution A neutral.

c The children should look up 'pH' in science dictionaries and then see if they can answer the questions on the Extend sheet.

OUTCOMES

EXPECTED RESULTS

a If the sample liquids are as suggested in resources and setting up above, the white wine vinegar and fizzy lemonade should turn the litmus pink (acid). The washing soda should turn litmus blue (alkali) and the distilled water should produce no change to the litmus.

b The amount of liquid B that will need to be added to A will depend on the strengths of the solutions.

c The children can colour the pH scale according to the colours of universal indicator. This ranges from red at pH1 through the colours of the rainbow to purple for pH14. PH7 is a bluey green colour. The answers to the problems on the Extend sheet are as follows:

1 The pH of tap water may vary but should be close to neutral.
2 Lemon juice will be somewhere in the range 0–7.
3 Washing up liquid is usually mildly alkali (about 8 or 9).
4 pH 7 is neutral.
5 pH 1 is very acidic.
6 pH 3 is weakly acidic.
7 pH 12 is quite strongly alkaline.

WATCHPOINTS

⚠️ Remind the children of the care they must take with experimental liquids and that they should on no account deliberately inhale or taste them, and that they should avoid getting them on their hands.

● Try out experiment **b** before the class, and then give all the work groups similar solutions. The expected outcomes will then be known to the teacher.

Assessment of learning outcomes

a Help sheet.

b Workbook page.

c Extend sheet.

Separating mixtures

Learning intentions

a Know what is meant by filtering a mixture.

b Separate some mixtures.

c Know of ways sieving and filtering are used in the kitchen.

Vocabulary

Filtering, mixture

Lesson pattern

Whole class and Help sheet, teacher demonstration, practical work and Workbook page, Extend sheet

RESOURCES AND SETTING UP

a Help sheet.

b Workbook page. A beaker containing iron filings and sand, a beaker containing iron filings and water, a beaker containing salt and water, bar magnet, funnel, clamp and stand with filter paper (or a funnel with filter paper, balanced in the neck of a beaker), shallow dish.

For each work group: a beaker containing sand and water, a funnel, a clamp and stand, a spoon, filter paper, an empty beaker.

ACTIVITIES

INTRODUCTION

 Ask the children what they understand by filtering and why we need to filter things. Show the children the equipment necessary for filtering. Hand out copies of the Help sheet and discuss it with the children.

a Following the introduction, show the children the four experimental beakers. Explain that they are going to be shown how to separate the mixture of iron filings and sand, the mixture of iron filings and water and the mixture of salt and water. They themselves will be given the chance to separate the mixture of sand and water.

Use the bar magnet to retrieve the iron filings from the sand. Stir the iron filing and water mixture with a non-metal spoon, then filter the iron filings out of the water and leave the filter paper to dry. Set a shallow dish containing the salt water on a warm window sill, and remind the children to predict what will happen and look at it from time to time over the coming week.

b In their work groups the children should report on the experiments already done and filter their mixture of sand and water and record the results of this on the Workbook page.

c Ask the children to comment on the images of sieving and filtering on the Extend sheet.

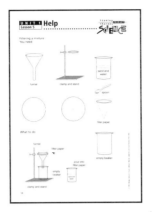

OUTCOMES

EXPECTED RESULTS

a Following the introduction the children should understand what is meant by filtering.

b Results on the Workbook page should retell what the teacher did in the demonstration and record the successful filtering of the sand and water.

c The filtering and sieving examples shown on the Extend sheet are as follows: (1) coffee, (2) flour, (3) sugar, (4) dirt and food scraps in the sink, (5) tea, (6) water, (7) boiled vegetables, (8) food scraps in the dishwasher.

WATCHPOINTS

● Take great care to handle iron filings in a plastic tray or other suitable container, so that they do not spill. They are difficult to collect, and once magnetised could affect watches, calculators, computers and other electronic equipment.

 Warn the children not to get filings on their fingers, as they could cause injury if accidentally rubbed in the eye or mouth.

Assessment of learning outcomes

a Participation in the introduction and the Workbook page.

b Workbook page.

c Extend sheet.

'Hands on' mixture separation

Learning intentions

a Know about the use of a magnet, filtering and evaporation in separating some mixtures.

b Separate a mixture of iron filings, sand and water.

c Find out how sea salt reaches our tables.

Vocabulary

Filter, separate

Lesson pattern

Whole class, practical work and Workbook page, research and Extend sheet

RESOURCES AND SETTING UP

b Workbook page. For each work group the following are required: a beaker containing iron filings, sand and salt, a jug of water, a bar magnet, a funnel, a clamp and stand, a spoon, filter paper, an empty beaker.

c Extend sheet. Encyclopaedias and other resources containing information about sea salt.

ACTIVITIES

INTRODUCTION

● Tell the children that they are going to have the chance in this lesson to separate a mixture using what they learned in the last lesson. Show the children the shallow dish which contained the salt water and was left out after the last lesson. Even if the water has not all evaporated there should be the start of some salt crystals forming at the edge of the saucer. Ask the children to recall how the iron filings, sand and salt were separated out in the previous lesson. Tell them that all three things are in the mixture they are working with, and they should be careful to work out the order of what they do before trying the experiment.

a The children should join in the introductory discussion.

b In their work groups the children should carry through the experiment to separate the iron filings, sand and salt. They should record their work on the Workbook page.

c The children are asked here to find out what happens to sea salt to make it ready for the table, recording their findings on the Extend sheet.

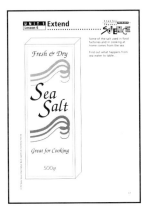

OUTCOMES

EXPECTED RESULTS

a Following the introduction the children should know about the use of a magnet, filtering and evaporation in separating the sample mixtures used in the previous lesson.

b The children should opt to take the filings out with a magnet, add water and filter out the sand and then leave the salt water to evaporate.

c Research should reveal that sea salt is extracted by an evaporation process.

WATCHPOINTS

• Children need to be carefully supervised in using the magnet on iron filings. (See the Watchpoints for the previous lesson.) Magnets also should be kept away from watches, calculators, computers and other electronic equipment.

Assessment of learning outcomes

a Involvement in this and the previous lesson.

b Workbook page.

c Extend sheet.

Changes

Learning intentions

a Revise the nature of reversible and irreversible change.

b Conduct an irreversible change.

c Puzzle out some reversible and irreversible changes.

Vocabulary

Change, irreversible, reversible

Lesson pattern

Whole class (possibly demonstration), Help sheet, practical work and Workbook page, Extend sheet

RESOURCES AND SETTING UP

a Help sheet. If the children have completed Year 3/P4 of this course they should have some knowledge of reversible and irreversible change. If it is necessary to repeat demonstrations, here are some suggested resources taken from Year 3/P4, Unit 3: clay or other modelling material and access to a kiln or oven (models from this material should be made before the lesson); two ice cube trays, water, access to a freezer before the lesson in order to make ice cubes in one of the trays; night light candle, candlestick, matches, protected surface and tin tray for the candle.

b Workbook page. Ask each child to bring an empty food tub, e.g. margarine or yoghurt carton. Small clay or Plasticine slab for each child, objects to make imprints in the clay, large quantity of plaster of Paris with instructions, large bowl, stirrer, water.

c Extend sheet.

ACTIVITIES

INTRODUCTION

● Show the children the ice cube tray with ice cubes in it, and a similar tray with water in it. Talk about what happens to ice when left in the warm. Discuss the change from water to ice and back again. Make sure the children understand the reversibility of the change. Light the candle and drip some hot wax onto a metal plate or other non-flammable surface. Let the children watch what happens to the wax. (The candle should be kept on a tin tray at all times.)

a The children should watch and talk about the above demonstrations, and what happens to clay models when fired. They can complete the Help sheet.

b It may be appropriate to allow the children to do this activity in another session, a day or so before this lesson. Then they can look at the outcomes and write up the report in the lesson itself on the Workbook page.

The children should press a reasonably thick layer of Plasticine into the bottom of their margarine tubs and make the surface of it flat. They should then push an object into the surface of the Plasticine to leave a strong imprint.

Make up the plaster of Paris following the instructions on the wrapper. Allow the children to feel the outside of the bowl. It should feel warm, indicating that a chemical change is taking place. Tip the bowl's contents onto the children's clay 'moulds' inside their tubs so as to form a layer a couple of centimetres thick. Set aside all the tubs overnight.

c Allow the children to complete the change wordsearch puzzle on the Extend sheet.

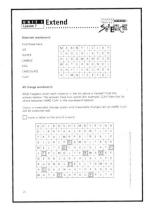

OUTCOMES

EXPECTED RESULTS

 The children should recall that reversible changes can be 'undone' and irreversible ones are chemical and permanent.

On the Help sheet they could include, for example:
(1) reversible – ice, wax, chocolate, jelly, water; and (2) irreversible – clay, cooked egg, bread or cake making, made up custard, toast.

b The changes that occur when water is added to powder like plaster of Paris render it hard and brittle. This is an irreversible change.

c The puzzle answers are as follows (see also next column):

				C	L	A	y
C	H	O	C	O	L	A	T	E
					N		
W	A	T	E	R		D		E
						L		G
				I	C	E		G

The following should be coloured green: melted chocolate, molten wax, water, water vapour.
The following should be coloured red: set egg, hard clay.

WATCHPOINTS

⚠ Take care with matches, naked flames and hot wax. Children need reminding not to approach the oven while models are baking. They should never be allowed near a pottery kiln while firing.

● Extra adult help would be invaluable for this lesson as plaster of Paris starts to set quite quickly. The implements and bowls also need washing thoroughly straight after use and residues should be disposed of safely, or the plaster of Paris may prove difficult to remove.

					H						
					A						
					R						
	S				D						
M	E	L	T	E	D	C	H	O	C	O	L	A	T	E
	T		M	O	L	T	E	N	W	A	X
	E				A				A		
	G				y				T		
	G								E		
W	A	T	E	R	V	A	P	O	U	R	

Assessment of learning outcomes

a Help sheet.

b Practical work and Workbook page.

c Extend sheet.

Saturation

Learning intentions

a Know what a saturated solution is.

b Make a saturated solution.

c Compare saturated solutions.

Vocabulary

Saturate, saturated, saturation, solute, solvent

Lesson pattern

Whole class demonstration, practical work and Workbook page, Extend sheet

RESOURCES AND SETTING UP

a Beaker half full of cold water with some sugar dissolved in it, sugar, spoon.

b Workbook page. For each work group:

beaker half full of cold water, beaker half full of warm water (all beakers should contain the same volume of water), substances to add to the water; half the groups should have sugar and the other half salt, teaspoon.

c Extend sheet. Access to the results of another work group.

ACTIVITIES

INTRODUCTION

● Tell the children that a saturated solution is one in which no more of the substance that has been dissolved (solute) will dissolve in the liquid (solvent). Show the children the sugar solution in the beaker. Add more sugar, a level teaspoonful at a time, and stir each time. When sugar crystals remain in the solution after stirring announce that the solution is saturated.

a The children should view the teacher demonstration and listen to the explanation.

b In their work groups the children should conduct an experiment to make a saturated solution, using beakers of cold and then of warm water. They can record their experiment on the Workbook page.

c Those children who finish writing up activity **b** can compare their results with those of a group who produced a different solution and tabulate both their own and the other group's results to offer comparisons on the Extend sheet.

OUTCOMES

EXPECTED RESULTS

a It is expected that the children will understand what saturation is when they have seen the demonstration.

b The results will be determined by, for example, the water temperature or the kind of sugar. There should be little variation between groups in the same class, providing they are working with similar materials under similar conditions. It is likely that more solute will dissolve in the warm water before saturation is reached.

c The children may find that results differ for different solutes.

Assessment of learning outcomes

a Attention to the demonstration.

b Workbook page.

c Extend sheet.

Soils, rocks and minerals

Learning intentions

a Know what soils, rocks and minerals are.

b Group rocks according to characteristics.

c Know how different rocks came to be formed.

Vocabulary

Characteristic, igneous, mineral rock, sedimentary, soil

Lesson pattern

Whole class workshop and Help sheet, practical work and Workbook page, research and Extend sheet

RESOURCES AND SETTING UP

a Help sheet. Poster 1.9. Soil samples, rock samples and mineral samples, all appropriately labelled and placed on display together with books about minerals and the Earth's structure. If possible the samples can be spread around the room for the lesson, so that all the children have a chance to take a good look. Examples of minerals include: quartz, mica and rock salt.

b Workbook page. For each work group: a box of rock samples to include at least three of different appearance and characteristics, magnifiers.

c Extend sheet. Books about sedimentary and igneous rocks.

ACTIVITIES

INTRODUCTION

● Point out the samples of soils, rocks and minerals. Check that the children know what these are, and that they come from the Earth itself. Check that they can distinguish a rock from a mineral. A rock is any solid material forming part of the Earth. Rocks contain minerals. Minerals are therefore found in the ground and have specific composition and properties. Invite the children to inspect the samples.

a The children should listen carefully to the introduction and then view the sample soils, rocks and minerals on display. They can record their observations on the Help sheet.

b In their work groups the children should look carefully at the rock samples in their study box, choose three of them and draw and write about their observations on the Workbook page.

c The children should find out from books and other sources, what igneous and sedimentary rocks are, and record definitions on the Extend sheet. If there is time they can look again at the samples in the classroom and see if they can say which are likely to be igneous and which sedimentary.

OUTCOMES

EXPECTED RESULTS

a Following the introduction and inspection of the samples the children should distinguish soil, rocks and minerals.

b The outcomes will depend on the examples inspected but the children should be able to describe the samples according to some of these characteristics: colour, shape (smooth, jagged, spiky), size of particles in it, softness (does dust flake off?), hardness, 'weight' in comparison with other samples.

c Igneous rocks are made when rock from inside the Earth, at such high temperatures and pressures that it is runny, is forced onto the Earth's surface where it cools. This can happen in earthquakes and volcanic eruptions. Basalt and granite are examples.

Sedimentary rocks are those formed when particles settle in layers, either through chemical action or the decay of living things. For example, trees from millions of years ago died and eventually turned into coal. Sand that settles will, over a long time scale, become sandstone.

WATCHPOINTS

● Metamorphic rocks have not been mentioned here. They are rocks near the sites of volcanic activity which have been heated and changed by the volcanic activity.

Assessment of learning outcomes

a Participation in the introduction and the Help sheet.

b Workbook page.

c Extend sheet.

Investigating soil

Learning intentions

a Inspect a sample of soil.

b Test soils for permeability.

c Know what a pH soil test does.

Vocabulary

Permeability, pH, soil

Lesson pattern

Whole class,
practical work in groups
and Help sheet,
practical work in groups
and Workbook page,
research and Extend sheet

RESOURCES AND SETTING UP

a Help sheet. For each work group: a shallow tray of surface soil (freshly dug), magnifiers, plastic gloves (or clear plastic bags to use as gloves), lolly sticks or 'dibbers', sorting trays, 'bug' boxes, white card and other display materials.

b Workbook page. For each work group: two different soil samples (for example, one could be very sandy and the other a bulb planting medium or clay soil), about a cup full of each soil will be plenty, a plastic spoon, funnel, filter papers, clamps and stands (a funnel could be balanced on a beaker if clamps and stands are not available), beakers, jugs of water, and a measuring jug or cylinder, timer or watch with a minute hand.

c Extend sheet. For each work group:

a soil test kit, or information about such a kit books about garden plants.

ACTIVITIES

INTRODUCTION

● Tell the children that their first task is to inspect a soil sample carefully. Remind the children that they should wear protective gloves while handling the soil.

a In their work groups the children should look carefully at the soil, then draw and write down what they find on the Help sheet. The lolly sticks can be used for sifting through the soil. They should identify what they think is in the sample.

b Using the filtering process that they are now familiar with, the children should set up the funnel with filter paper over a beaker. A number of spoonfuls of soil should be placed in the paper (four or five). A measured amount of water should be poured carefully on the soil (perhaps 10 or 15 ml). The group should look on and one person should time how long it takes for the water to stop dripping through. The timing can continue until the drips are more than two minutes apart and then stop. The results should be recorded on the Workbook page and the second soil sample treated in the same way.

c The children should use the knowledge of pH they may have gained in Lesson 4 in this unit and find out more about soils that are acid or alkali.

OUTCOMES

EXPECTED RESULTS

a The children may find a wide variety of things in the soil including leaves, pebbles, twigs, biodegradable waste like paper or matchsticks, other waste like plastic, seeds, mini beasts. The intention is that they should recognise that soil is not homogeneous.

b The children should reveal that soils differ in the rate at which water is allowed through (or the extent to which they retain water).

c A soil test is used by gardeners so that they can determine which kinds of plants will grow best, or what additions should be made to soil to change its pH.

Plants that tolerate acid soils include camellias, rhododendrons and heathers. Plants that tolerate alkaline soils include hydrangeas and roses.

WATCHPOINTS

⚠ Ensure that any cuts or scratches that the children have on their hands are covered with a plaster and/or gloves when handling the soil. All children should wash their hands with soap and water at the end of the activity. After the lesson the soil samples should be returned to their original site, along with any mini beasts found in the soil.

Assessment of learning outcomes

a Help sheet.

b Workbook page.

c Extend sheet.

Firework safety

Learning intentions

a Know the firework safety code.

b Recognise firework dangers.

c Create firework safety slogans.

Vocabulary

Explosion, firework, Guy Fawkes, Gunpowder

Lesson pattern

Whole class, Help sheet, Workbook page, Extend sheet

RESOURCES AND SETTING UP

- Poster 1.11.

- No resources are essential but it may be helpful to have information about firework accidents, and firework packaging, to augment the introduction to the lesson.

a Help sheet.

b Workbook page.

c Extend sheet.

ACTIVITIES

INTRODUCTION

- Using Poster 1.11, indicate to the children the main points of the firework code.

- Explain what is celebrated on 5 November. Give the children accident details and statistics (current ones if these are available). Point out that the substances in the fireworks are of the kind that is explosive when heated or burned

a Invite the children to write out the points in the firework code on the Help sheet.

b Using the Workbook page the children should inspect the picture where all the dangers are tagged and write down the nature of each danger.

c The children are invited to invent a safety slogan, jingle or rhyme and write it on the Extend sheet.

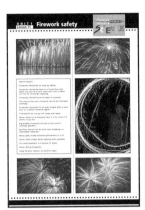

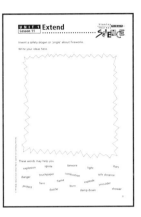

OUTCOMES

EXPECTED RESULTS

a Work on the Help sheet should be checked. The children can check each other's work. The points made should match those made in the introduction.

b The seven dangers on the Workbook page are as follows:

1 The bonfire is unbalanced and very high.
2 Someone is too close to the fire.
3 Someone has a burning stick.
4 The lid is off the firework box.
5 Someone has a sparkler and no gloves.
6 There is a building close by.
7 The onlookers are too close to the fireworks.

c This could be very simple and still have a great deal of impact. For example, 'Get excited but not ignited!'

WATCHPOINTS

● The children cannot be over informed about the nature of the materials found in fireworks and their potential dangers.

Assessment of learning outcomes

a Help sheet.

b Workbook page.

c Extend sheet.

Review

RESOURCES AND SETTING UP

● Adjust seating arrangements to test conditions.

a **b** Workbook pages 1 and 2.

c Extend sheet. Poster 1.9, books about rocks and minerals.

ACTIVITIES

Ask the children to complete the Workbook pages. Those who finish can, using Poster 1.9 and school resources respond to the challenge on the Extend sheet.

WATCHPOINTS

● Remind the children that they can also complete their own checklist about the unit when they have time. The checklist can be found at the end of the material for this unit in the photocopiable resources.

OUTCOMES

EXPECTED ANSWERS

● Answers to the Extend sheet will depend on the rock or mineral chosen and the resources accessed.

UNIT 1 Review Workbook — Stanley Thornes PRIMARY Science

1 List two uses for a flexible material.
   (some examples) soft furnishing / clothing /

2 This table knife has a wooden handle and metal blade. Why are wood and metal used?
   Wooden handle because _wood is hard / attractive / cheap / can be made into shape_
   Metal blade because _metal can be made in 'thin slice' with a sharp edge / metal is flexible not brittle so will not break in use / metal can be cleaned easily_

3 What is an acid indicator?
   a substance that shows by a colour change that a solution is acid

4 What colour does litmus go when dipped in acid? _____ pink

5 Which would you use to separate these mixtures?
   Sand and water _funnel and filter paper_   magnet
   Sand and iron filings _____ magnet
   funnel and filter paper

6 Which of these changes is irreversible? tick ✓
   Boiling an egg [✓]
   Baking a clay model [✓]
   Melting candle wax [ ]
   Making plaster of Paris [✓]

32

UNIT 1 Review Workbook — Stanley Thornes PRIMARY Science

7 When a substance dissolves in a liquid we make a _____ solution.
   When no more substance will dissolve in the liquid we make a _____ saturated _____ solution.

8 Where does rock come from? _____ the Earth itself
   What is a mineral? _a mineral comes from the ground but has special properties and composition_

9 Why do gardeners need to know whether the soil is permeable?
   soil which is not permeable can retain too much water which may affect plants / rot plant roots / cause plants to die

10 List two ways fireworks can be dangerous.
   lit fireworks can burn you
   fireworks can set fire to things
   the contents of fireworks can explode

33

ABOUT THIS UNIT

This unit is an introduction to some of the major body systems and how they work. Beginning with the importance of rest and exercise for human beings, there are links to lesson 2 in which the children learn about how we breathe and our circulatory system. Lessons 3 and 4 allow children to learn more about health and nutrition and this includes the main steps in digestion, which will be investigated further at Key Stage 3. There follows a lesson about hygiene which links to the need for cleanliness in handling food and after using the lavatory. These ideas may well have arisen during the previous two lessons.

Drugs can be dangerous; they are often within reach of children. The focus in this school year is on smoking and alcohol. The second half of the unit is about body systems in animals other than humans. The children study respiration, the main organs in fish, animal eating habits and species where body shape and size is adapted for social role (the social insects). The final lesson allows children to enlarge their knowledge of animal reproduction by learning about egg layers.

SPECIAL RESOURCES AND ADVANCED PLANNING

Lesson 1
An expert on rest and exercise is required to give a short talk. For the Extend activity parental permission about keeping a diary on rest and exercise will be required.

Lesson 2
Watches or a clock with a minute hand are required.

Lesson 3
A basket of shopping, food packaging and old menu cards are required.

Lesson 5
The school cook or kitchen worker should talk to the children about the importance of hygiene in the kitchen.

Lesson 6
Leaflets and information about drugs and their abuse.

Lesson 7
A whole fresh fish bought from the fishmonger would be invaluable here.

Lesson 9
A bird table is required.

Lesson 10
Live ants for the children to examine would be useful and would enhance the children's learning but are not essential.

BOOK AND MULTIMEDIA SEARCH

Human body systems:
    respiratory system,
    circulatory system,
    digestive system.

Drugs
Animal body systems
Animal diets/eating habits
Social insects
Eggs and egg layers

UNIT MAP

Lesson 1
A Know that humans need rest and exercise.
b Know why humans need rest and exercise.
c Keep a diary of rest and exercise.

Lesson 2
A Know that breathing and heart rate are affected by exercise.
b Know about respiration and the circulatory system.
c Know what the 'pulse' is and try taking it.

Lesson 3
A Know what the main food groups are and why we need a balanced diet.
b Know about the nutritional content of some foods.
c Know of the value and source of some vitamins and minerals.

Lesson 4
A Know what digestion means.
b Describe the main steps in ingestion, digestion and egestion.
c Learn some of the vocabulary and facts and figures relating to the alimentary canal.

Lesson 5
A Know about hygiene in the kitchen.
b Know the rules of personal hygiene.
c Spot germ risk areas in the home.

Lesson 6
A Know what a drug is.
b Know about drug abuse.
c Draw a poster telling children and young people that drugs are harmful.

Lesson 7
A Know that all vertebrates 'breathe' and have circulatory systems.
b Know of similarities and differences between animal groups regarding breathing and blood.
c Find out about the body systems of invertebrates.

Lesson 8
A Know that fish get their oxygen from the water around them.
b Know how the gills work.
c Find out about fish body systems.

Lesson 9
A Know that animals' eating habits and digestion differ from species to species.
b Know about eating and digestion in some animals.
c Investigate what garden birds like to eat.

Lesson 10
A Know that some creatures live in colonies where individuals have different structures and tasks.
b Know about the social organisation of ants.
c Create an ant fact book.

Lesson 11
A Know that all animals produce eggs, and that most species 'lay' the eggs where they develop outside the parent's body.
b Know about the sequence of events in the development of the chick.
c Identify some bird eggs.

UNIT 2
Body works

LESSON 1

Rest and exercise

Learning intentions

a Know that humans need rest and exercise.

b Know why humans need rest and exercise.

c Keep a diary of rest and exercise.

Vocabulary

Active, exercise, relaxation, rest, sleep, strenuous

Lesson pattern

Whole class talk and demonstration, Workbook page, practical work and Extend sheet

RESOURCES AND SETTING UP

● Invite a visiting expert to talk to the children about the importance of rest and exercise. The expert needs to have an interest in the physiology of sport. Some suggested contact points are: the Sports Council, secondary school PE departments, colleges with sports science departments, health clubs. The expert should talk for a maximum of 30 minutes, including a discussion of the importance of rest and exercise, and the effects of different kinds of exercise on the body.

b Workbook page.

c Extend sheet.

ACTIVITIES

INTRODUCTION

● Introduce the topic to the children. Ask them what they think human beings need. They may say things like food, shelter and love. Confirm that they all know that humans need adequate rest and exercise in order to stay healthy. Introduce the speaker to the children.

a The children should take part in the introductory discussion.

b The children should listen to the speaker and then try to answer the questions related to rest and exercise on the Workbook page.

c Those children who complete the Workbook page should begin a diary about rest and exercise using the Extend sheet. They should start with the day of the lesson and complete it at home over the week that follows the lesson.

OUTCOMES

EXPECTED RESULTS

a The children should understand that adequate rest (especially sleep) is essential to physical and mental health and that exercise helps in both these respects too.

b The answers the children write on the Workbook page will depend on the points made by the visiting speaker.

c The diary entries will depend on individual children's lifestyle. Comparisons of outcomes may provoke further discussion about individual differences as well as optimal levels of rest and exercise.

WATCHPOINTS

● It may be helpful to take notes while the visitor talks, so that what the children have learned can be consolidated. Key words used by the speaker may be helpful.

● The **c** activity could be done by all the children. This will provide a data bank for secondary analysis, class discussion or inspiration for work in other areas of the curriculum, e.g. drama or art.

Assessment of learning outcomes

a Participation and attention in the early part of the lesson.

b Workbook page.

c Extend sheet.

Breathing and blood circulation

Learning intentions

a Know that breathing and heart rate are affected by exercise.

b Know about respiration and the circulatory system.

c Know what the 'pulse' is and try taking it.

Vocabulary

Arteries, breathing, carbon dioxide, circulatory system, heart, lungs, oxygen, respiration, veins

Lesson pattern

Whole class and demonstration, Workbook page, practical work and Extend sheet

RESOURCES AND SETTING UP

- Charts and pictures showing how we breathe and our blood circulatory system.
- Watch or clock with a second hand.

b Workbook page.

c Extend sheet.

ACTIVITIES

INTRODUCTION

- Remind the children of the work they did on breathing in Year 4/P5. Check that the children understand that we need oxygen from the air in order to live. The oxygen is required to help our bodies get energy from the food we eat.

- Show the children the important steps in respiration. Include the points made on the Workbook page, emphasizing that the blood system is the 'transport' or circulatory system of the body. Oxygen is carried in the blood to all parts of the body by the arteries. Waste carbon dioxide is carried away from all parts of the body by the veins. The blood from the veins is pumped by the heart to the lungs, where it picks up a fresh supply of oxygen, returns to the heart and is pumped from there around the body through the arteries.

a Ask a volunteer to stand up and breathe normally. If the child runs on the spot for about two minutes, the children looking on will see that the breathing rate quickens and the child should be able to detect that the heart rate has got faster too.

b Following the introduction and demonstration the children should be able to complete the Workbook page about breathing and circulation.

c Invite the children to find out about the 'pulse' using the Extend sheet.

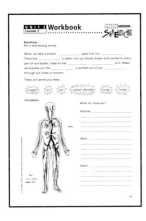

OUTCOMES

EXPECTED RESULTS

a The experiment should show the children that our breathing rate and heart rate are linked. During exercise the working muscles need more oxygen. We breathe quicker to take in more oxygen and the heart beats quicker to deliver more oxygen to the muscles.

b The Workbook page should read like this:

- Breathing – missing words are air, lungs, oxygen, carbon dioxide, air, lungs.
- Circulation – arteries carry blood with oxygen in it away from the lungs, and away from the heart to all parts of the body.
- Veins carry blood that has lost oxygen, and has carbon dioxide in it, to the lungs and to the heart from all parts of the body.
- The heart is a muscular pump for the blood, sending it to the lungs to get oxygen and to the body parts to supply oxygen.

c The children should, with the help of the Extend sheet and a watch with a second hand, be able to find their own pulse rate and compare it with that of a friend.

WATCHPOINTS

⚠ No child who is excused PE should take part in the breathing/heart experiment in activity **a**.

Assessment of learning outcomes

a Attention to the introduction and demonstration.

b Workbook page.

c Extend sheet.

Food and health

Learning intentions

a Know what the main food groups are and why we need a balanced diet.

b Know about the nutritional content of some foods.

c Know of the value and source of some vitamins and minerals.

Vocabulary

Balance, carbohydrate, diet, energy, fat, fibre, minerals, protein, sugar, vitamins

Lesson pattern

Whole class, Help sheets, Workbook page, Extend sheet.

RESOURCES AND SETTING UP

a Help sheets 1 and 2. If it is possible to arrange, a basket of shopping, including some of the items on the Help sheet would be useful. Pictures of food and food packaging listing ingredients.

b Workbook page.

c Extend sheet. Menu cards from cafés and restaurants are not essential but the children may be interested to look at and compare them with one another and with the menu the children themselves devise.

ACTIVITIES

INTRODUCTION

● Remind the children of their work in Year 3/P4 of this course. See if they can recall why we eat, why we eat a variety of foods and the main food groups. Using the Help sheet, tell the children about the food groups listed. Fibre is also important to health. Our bodies do not take in fibre but it is bulky and helps our 'food system' or digestive system work properly. Talk about the foods in the shopping basket and the nutrients they contain.

● Mention to the children that the lack of a balanced diet can lead to ill-health. (See Watchpoints.)

a Hand out the Help sheets and talk through the nutrients available in the different foods. Note that some mineral sources are listed on the Extend sheet. Ask the children to cut out the foods from Help sheet 2 and stick them in the correct group on Help sheet 1.

b Invite the children to complete the Workbook page using their Help sheet and what has been said in the lesson so far to help them.

c Using the vitamin and mineral chart on the Extend sheet and their own knowledge of food, the children are asked to create a nutritious vitamin- and mineral-rich three course menu. If there are sample menus available, let the children look at these for inspiration and comparison.

OUTCOMES

EXPECTED RESULTS

 It is expected that the foods will be placed as follows:

- carbohydrates: wholemeal bread, cereals, cakes, biscuits, potatoes.
- proteins: fish, meat, beans, peas, cheese, milk, yogurt.
- fats: cooking oil, spread, butter.
- vitamins and minerals: fruit, vegetables.

Note that many of these foods contain a range of nutrients, and could therefore be assigned to other groups. They are listed here, in the groups to which they make a strong contribution.

b The children's Workbook page answers should include these points:

- cereal: carbohydrate (starch), fibre
- eggs: protein
- fruit and juices: vitamins (especially C)
- salad: vitamins and minerals
- fish and meat: proteins
- milk: proteins and minerals (especially calcium)

The following points should also be made:

- For healthy bones and teeth we need foods containing calcium (milk and milk products) and vitamin D (fish).
- For plenty of energy we need carbohydrate-rich foods like bread and cereals.
- Vitamins are good for the eyes and skin.
- Iron keeps our red blood cells healthy.

c The menu the children create should be novel, but they should be able to justify their choice of foods on nutritional grounds.

WATCHPOINTS

● Tell the children that it is not just people who do not eat enough (like those who are victims of natural disasters or war) who become unwell. There are people in wealthy nations who through poverty cannot have a healthy diet, or ignorance do not know how to eat healthily. There may even be malnourished children in the school or class.

Assessment of learning outcomes

a Help sheet 1 (with foods stuck on).

b Workbook page.

c Extend sheet.

Digestion

Learning intentions

a Know what digestion means.

b Describe the main steps in ingestion, digestion and egestion.

c Learn some of the vocabulary and facts and figures relating to the alimentary canal.

Vocabulary

Circulatory system, digestion, excretory system, juices, large intestine, nutrients, oesophagus, rectum, small intestine, stomach

Lesson pattern

Whole class, Workbook page, Extend sheet and practical work

RESOURCES AND SETTING UP

a Charts and diagrams showing the main parts of the digestive system.

b Help sheet and Workbook page.

c Extend sheet. Work groups will need: access to a tap, measuring jugs and bowls, roll of lining paper, measuring tapes.

ACTIVITIES

INTRODUCTION

● Find out what the children know about what happens to food once they have put it into their mouths. Add any of the following points that the children themselves do not make:

- all creatures need to take in nutrients and get rid of waste.
- we need nutrients in order to live.
- we get nutrients from food.
- the food we eat helps us grow, stay healthy and gives us energy.
- food is taken into our bodies through our mouths.
- while inside us food makes a journey into our stomachs and abdomens. Along the way it is broken down so that the nutrients can be taken into the body.

a The children should listen to and participate in the introduction to the lesson.

b Hold up a copy of the Help sheet and the Workbook page. Discuss what happens to our food inside us, and show the children the relevant parts of the diagrams they will be working with. These are the points to make:

- saliva mixes with the food while we chew and when soft we swallow.
- the food goes down a tube called the oesophagus into the stomach.
- in the stomach it is mixed with more digestive juices and broken down further.
- it then passes into the intestine which is a very, very long tube.
- as it is moved along by the action of the muscles in the tube wall it is made into very small particles.
- the goodness from this passes into the body and the undigested material is collected at the end of the tube, called the rectum.
- when we go to the lavatory we get rid of this waste.

The children can then cut up the Help sheet and stick the parts on the Workbook page.

c The children should look at the data on the Extend sheet and measure out the liquid quantities using a measuring jug and the lengths on a roll of lining paper. These can be put on display.

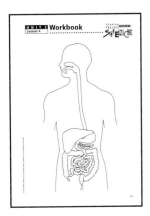

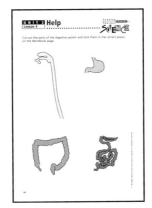

OUTCOMES

EXPECTED RESULTS

a Participation in the introductory discussion should mean the children understand what digestion is.

b Following the discussion the children should be able to stick the organs in the correct places on the diagram.

c The children may be surprised at the sheer length of our alimentary canal.

WATCHPOINTS

● This is a lesson in which there are many technical words to use. This lesson should set the scene for work done at KS3, and so it is more important that the children begin to understand the process of digestion than learn all the vocabulary.

● If the children are very well informed they can also be helped to understand the roles of the kidneys and the circulatory system in getting rid of waste (via the bladder and lungs).

Assessment of learning outcomes

a Participation in the introduction.

b Workbook page (with parts from the Help sheet stuck on).

c Extend sheet and accompanying practical work.

Hygiene

Learning intentions

a Know about hygiene in the kitchen.

b Know the rules of personal hygiene.

c Spot germ risk areas in the home.

Vocabulary

Disease, germs, hygiene

Lesson pattern

Whole class,
Help sheet,
whole class,
Workbook page,
Extend sheet

RESOURCES AND SETTING UP

- Invite the school cook or a member of the kitchen staff to come and talk to the children about hygiene rules.

a Help sheet.

b Poster 2.5. Workbook page.

c Extend sheet.

ACTIVITIES

INTRODUCTION

- Tell the children that the lesson is about hygiene, and that hygiene roughly means keeping clean. Introduce the speaker.

a The visitor should tell the children the hygiene regulations that everyone must abide by in the kitchen, and the children can then try to complete the Help sheet.

b Gather the children together and discuss with them what they should do regarding personal hygiene. Show the children Poster 2.5. Talk about, for example, washing hands after going to the lavatory, cleaning teeth, having all over washes, showers or baths regularly, washing hands before handling food, regular hair washing, use of soap to remove grease and keeping nails clean. Ask the children to use what they have learned to compile a 'Personal Hygiene Book' using the Workbook page.

c Invite the children to look at the cutaway house drawn on the Extend sheet and mark in where there might be problems about hygiene.

OUTCOMES

EXPECTED RESULTS

a The points the children make will depend on what the visitor says but may include the following:

- hands: washed before handling food, after handling waste or rubbish, after going to the lavatory
- hair: tucked out of the way, hat or headgear may be obligatory
- clothes: clean overalls, aprons
- cloths: separate for surfaces and floor, washed at boiling point
- surfaces: cleaned before and after each day's meals.

b The rules of personal hygiene that the children record should include the points made in activity **A** above.

c Things the children may spot include: the lavatory pan, the kitchen bin, the dog, the cat, the dustbin, the drains, the cat litter.

WATCHPOINTS

● The visitor should only talk for about ten or fifteen minutes concentrating on the rules and regulations governing behaviour in the school kitchen. If the school cook is unavailable other experts may be approached such as a chef or restaurateur, a school meals supervisor, a member of staff from the home economics department of a local college.

Assessment of learning outcomes

a Help sheet.

b Workbook page.

c Extend sheet.

Drugs

Learning intentions

a Know what a drug is.

b Know about drug abuse.

c Draw a poster telling children and young people that drugs are harmful.

Vocabulary

Alcohol, drug, tobacco, names of other drugs known to the children

Lesson pattern

Whole class and Help sheets,
Workbook page,
Extend sheet

RESOURCES AND SETTING UP

● Leaflets about drugs from health organisations.

a Help sheets 1 and 2.

b Workbook page.

c Extend sheet and poster-sized paper. Children's encyclopaedias which explain drug abuse in a straightforward way.

ACTIVITIES

INTRODUCTION

● It is important that the children should know what drugs are and to avoid abusing them, but the subject should be treated in a way that does not frighten them. In a whole class group go into activity **A**.

a In a whole class discussion talk about what a drug is and the kinds of drugs there are. Tell the children what 'abuse' is, hand out Help sheets 1 and 2 and talk these over. In this lesson the focus is on tobacco and alcohol. Solvents and other drugs are sometimes accessible to children and they should also be mentioned.

Here are some points to make to the children:

– solvents: these are constituents of things like paint, glue, aerosols and lighter fuel. The vapour when inhaled can make a person feel 'drunk'. Users can injure themselves, or cause lasting body damage.

– cannabis: usually smoked along with tobacco. It makes the taker feel relaxed. Its effects on the body are similar to those of tobacco.

Information about other drugs should also be sought by the teacher (see Watchpoints).

b The children should attempt to complete the Workbook page about drug facts, using the information they have gleaned from the class discussion and from the Help sheets.

c The children should use their knowledge to compile a 'tell all' fact sheet or poster to persuade children of the dangers of drugs.

OUTCOMES

EXPECTED RESULTS

 A drug is a substance made from plants or chemicals that has an effect on our bodies or minds. Some drugs are used to treat illness. When drugs are mis- or over-used this is called abuse.

b The answers to the challenges on the Workbook page are as follows.

Definitions of drugs, their use and misuse are set down in outcome **a** above. The drugs listed could be those mentioned in discussion or others the children know. Drug misuse can lead to injury and accident, addiction, crime (in order to support the habit), serious disease and death.

c The facts the children choose to use should include some of those mentioned in activities **a** and **b** above.

WATCHPOINTS

● This is a lesson to be handled with great care. There may be people in the children's own families who drink, smoke or take other drugs.

● It is important that the teacher secures detailed information about a wide range of drugs, so as to answer correctly questions the children may have. The booklet *Drugs and solvents: things you should know (the facts for young people)* prepared for the Department of Health and available through HMSO is useful. Health centres and libraries may have other similar publications.

● The material on the Help Sheet is taken from the *Guardian*, 9 March 1993, 'Smoking: every breath you take', by Mike Gilchrist, and is used by permission of the copyright holders.

Assessment of learning outcomes

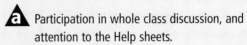

a Participation in whole class discussion, and attention to the Help sheets.

b Workbook page.

c Poster based on instructions on the Extend sheet.

Breathing and blood systems

Learning intentions

a Know that all vertebrates 'breathe' and have circulatory systems.

b Know of similarities and differences between animal groups regarding breathing and blood.

c Find out about the body systems of invertebrates.

Vocabulary

Blood circulation, breathing, circulatory, gills, lungs, respiration

Lesson pattern

Whole class and Help sheet,
Workbook page,
research and Extend sheet

RESOURCES AND SETTING UP

a Help sheet.

b Workbook page.

c Extend sheet. Books and other information about animal body systems including vertebrates and invertebrates

ACTIVITIES

INTRODUCTION

● Tell the children that the purpose in this lesson is to make comparisons between creatures, regarding the way they take in oxygen from air and their circulatory or transport systems. Hand out copies of the Help sheet and talk through it with the children. Point out to them that the groups of creatures represented are the five main groupings of vertebrates (that is animals with backbones). Remind the children of their work on these groupings in Years 3/P4 and 4/P5.

a The children should listen to the introduction and closely examine the Help sheet.

b Using the information on the Help sheet the children should complete the Workbook page.

c Using information books in the class and school library the children should find out about body systems in invertebrates.

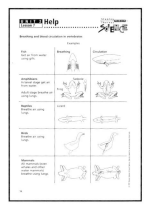

OUTCOMES

EXPECTED RESULTS

 The children should note that there are differences among the groups in their breathing mechanisms, but their circulatory systems have similarities.

b The Workbook entries should read as follows:

– mammals breathe air using lungs; amphibians get oxygen from water when they are tadpoles, as frogs they breathe air using lungs; fish have gills to help them breathe and get oxygen from water.
– amphibians; crested newt; lungs (in adult stage)
– mammals; Exmoor pony, grey seal, Daubenton's bat, water shrew, stoat; lungs
– fish; perch; gills
– reptile; sand lizard; lungs
– bird; jackdaw, buff Orpington hen; lungs.

c The notes the children make will depend on the sources they access.

WATCHPOINTS

● Note that the children will have an opportunity to study how fish breathe in greater detail in lesson 8.

Assessment of learning outcomes

a Participation in introductory part of the lesson.

b Workbook page.

c Extend sheet.

LESSON 8

Fish works

Learning intentions

a Know that fish get their oxygen from the water around them.

b Know how the gills work.

c Find out about fish body systems.

Vocabulary

Absorbed, blood vessels, gill covers, gills, oxygen

Lesson pattern

Whole class, Workbook page, Extend sheet

RESOURCES AND SETTING UP

● If possible, purchase a whole fresh fish to show the children. This will need to be wrapped and refrigerated before and after use in the lesson. If this is not available collect pictures of fish.

b Workbook page.

c Extend sheet. Books about fish.

ACTIVITIES

INTRODUCTION

● Remind the children that fish get oxygen from the water around them. Show the fresh fish or pictures of fish to the children. Point out the gills, and talk about what happens when the fish is swimming. The fish opens its mouth and water goes in. The gill covers are closed. The fish shuts its mouth, creating pressure inside. The gill covers open and the water streams out over the gills. The gills are well supplied with tiny blood vessels, and it is here that oxygen is absorbed into the blood system. Carbon dioxide diffuses into the water.

a The children should look at the fish or fish pictures and attend to the introduction.

b Invite the children to write a record of how fish breathe on the Workbook page.

c The children are required to inspect the bony fish diagram on the Extend sheet and find out about fish other than bony ones.

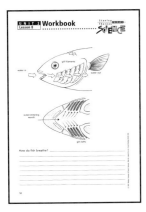

OUTCOMES

EXPECTED RESULTS

a The children should, after these two lessons, know that fish get oxygen from water.

b The children's explanation of how fish breathe should accord with that in the introduction above.

c Fish can be bony, cartilaginous or jawless; cartilaginous fish (e.g. sharks) lack swim bladders and have intestines that vary from bony fish; jawless fish (e.g. lampreys) have circular mouths with rasp-like teeth and have gill pouches rather than proper gills. The children may discover other differences between types of fish.

WATCHPOINTS

⚠ If children handle fish or fish material, make sure that they wash their hands with soap and water afterwards.

Assessment of learning outcomes

a Attention to the introduction.

b Attention to the introduction and record on the Workbook page.

c Extend sheet.

Animal eating habits

Learning intentions

a Know that the eating habits and digestion of animals differ from species to species.

b Know about eating and digestion in some animals.

c Investigate what garden birds like to eat.

Vocabulary

Bacteria, digestion, nutrients, ruminant, stomach

Lesson pattern

Whole class, Workbook page, practical work, Extend sheet

RESOURCES AND SETTING UP

a **b** Workbook page. Books about animals, their diets and eating habits.

c Extend sheet. This work may be done at home if appropriate and requires several short observation sessions, probably on different days. Useful items include: a bird table, a variety of foods suitable for birds, books about birds.

ACTIVITIES

INTRODUCTION

● Revise with the children what they now know about the diets of animals. They have worked on this in both Years 3/P4 and 4/P5. Ask if they can recall information about how food is digested.

a The children should join in the introductory discussion.

b Point out to the children that those animals that eat plants have some problems in getting the goodness out of their food. Plants are made of tiny parts called cells and the cell walls are made of cellulose. Cellulose is extremely tough and animals need to break through it to get nutrients from the plant cells. Different animals have a variety of ways of doing this. Here are some examples.

– The ruminants (e.g. cows) cut the grass with their front teeth. With the help of their tongue they then swallow it straight away. It goes into the rumen, which houses bacteria. The food moves about in here for some hours. Then it comes back into the mouth, a bit at a time, and is chewed up and down, side to side and forward and back. Then it is swallowed for a second time and goes into the stomach proper.

– The rabbit gets more nutrients from its plant diet by digesting the leaves in the normal way and then excreting soft pellets which the rabbit eats. These then go through the digestive tract again.

– By contrast meat is easier to digest, so the digestion of meat eaters needs little help, once the meat has been torn and chewed by the teeth.

The children can record some of the facts they have learned on the Workbook page.

c Using the school bird table or a bird table in their own or a neighbour's garden the children should investigate whether different birds eat different diets. The children can put different kinds of food on the table, either on different days or on different parts of the table. They should then log which birds eat which food and check it against reference material.

OUTCOMES

EXPECTED RESULTS

a What emerges in discussion depends on the children's recall of their work. For example, children who did activity **c** in Unit 1, Lesson 10 in Year 3/P4 may be able to tell the others about how cows digest their food. Those who did activity **c** in Unit 5, Lesson 3 in Year 4/P5 may be able to talk about birds regurgitating to feed their young.

b The answers on the Workbook page should match the facts raised in the activity above.

c Results here will depend on the garden birds common in the area of the school, the kinds of foods made available to them and the observation periods.

WATCHPOINTS

● Cooking makes the nutrients in vegetables more accessible to our bodies, and so it is possible for humans to have a nutritious diet without eating meat.

● If it is more appropriate for the children, activity **c** can be conducted as a class project over the winter months. It would be useful to erect a bird table that can be viewed from inside the classroom.

Assessment of learning outcomes

a Participation in the initial discussion.

b Completion of the Workbook page.

c Practical and recording work based on the Extend sheet.

Social insects

Learning intentions

a Know that some creatures live in colonies where individuals have different structures and tasks.

b Know about the social organisation of ants.

c Create an ant fact book.

Vocabulary

Ant, colony, function, queen, soldier, structure, wingless, worker

Lesson pattern

Whole class, Workbook page, Extend sheet

RESOURCES AND SETTING UP

- Poster 2.10.
- Books about ants.
- Information from an encyclopaedia about social insects.
- One or two ants in a 'bug box' or viewing container.

a **b** Workbook page.

c Extend sheet.

ACTIVITIES

INTRODUCTION

- Remind the children of the work they did on social insects in Unit 2 of Year 4/P5. Tell them that many kinds of creatures live in social groups. Some insects live in groups called colonies where individuals could not survive outside the group, and where they are different shapes and sizes and have different body structure according to the job they do for the colony. Important examples are wasps, bees and ants; and termites which have similar organisation to ants, but are not related to

them. If there are some specimen ants available let the children have a look at them under magnifiers.

a The children should attend to the introduction to the lesson.

b Tell the children that the focus here will be on ants and then give them the following facts:

- a single queen ant produces eggs.
- eggs hatch into ants that have no wings and cannot lay eggs.
- some of these ants are workers who forage for food and care for the queen and larvae.
- some of the ants are soldiers who protect the colony.
- male and female ants with wings are born into the colony when it is appropriate to leave the colony and start a new one.

Remind the children that these ants all look different from one another. Poster 2.10 shows the differences in the appearance of ants. The children should then complete the Workbook page.

c Ask the children to further investigate ants. The Extend sheet has some ant facts on it. The children can look for others and make an 'ant book' for classmates or other classes.

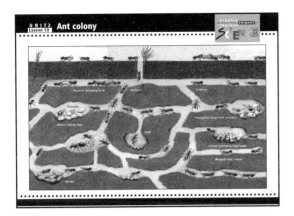

OUTCOMES

EXPECTED RESULTS

a The children should recall work about animals and social organisation.

b The children should learn the ant facts given them in activity **b**, and research their own if there is time.

c The Extend sheet facts should provide a starter list for ant books which can be displayed around the poster.

WATCHPOINTS

● Take care that ants do not escape from the viewing box. Ants can cause skin irritation. Be sure to return the ants to the location from which they came, after the lesson.

● If the children are very knowledgeable about ants, they can find out about termites instead.

Assessment of learning outcomes

a Attention to the introduction.

b Workbook page.

c 'Ant book' produced by the child.

Egg layers

Learning intentions

a Know that all animals produce eggs, and that most species 'lay' the eggs and they develop outside the parent's body.

b Know about the sequence of events in the development of the chick.

c Identify some bird eggs.

Vocabulary

Egg, female, fertilization, incubate, lay, male

Lesson pattern

Whole class, Help sheet, whole class, Help sheet and Workbook page, Extend sheet

RESOURCES AND SETTING UP

a **b** Help sheets 1 and 2 and Workbook page. Book about eggs, egg layers and animal reproduction.

c Extend sheet. Identification books about birds and their eggs.

ACTIVITIES

INTRODUCTION

● Tell the children that all animals including humans produce eggs. Most creatures lay their eggs and they develop into the young outside the animal's body. Mammals keep the eggs inside them where development takes place.

a Show the children Help sheet 1 and ask which creatures are there and which animal groups they belong to. Point out that all their eggs are there too. Give each child a copy of Help sheet 1. Talk through which animal is likely to go with each clutch of eggs and then invite the children to join each creature to the correct eggs. Give the children the correct match list so that they can modify their own version if necessary.

b Talk about the steps in chick development. The children can then cut out the pictures on Help sheet 2 and put them in the correct order on the Workbook page.

c Allow the children to consult the books about birds and identify the eggs on the Extend sheet. You may wish to give the children a short list of birds from which to choose to narrow the range of this activity.

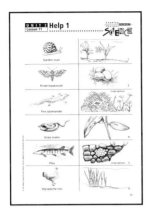

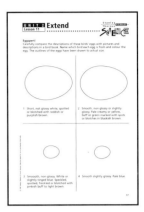

OUTCOMES

EXPECTED RESULTS

a The children should understand from the introduction that all animals produce eggs. The answers to the Help sheet are as follows: garden snail (mollusc), 5; moth (insect), 4; salamander (amphibian), 1; snake (reptile), 3; pike, 6; Wyandotte hen (bird), 2.

b The chick development pictures should be as follows.

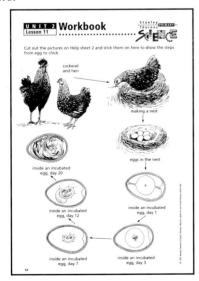

c The eggs are from the following species of birds: **1** red kite, **2** black-headed gull, **3** robin, **4** pied flycatcher.

WATCHPOINTS

● This lesson is intended to set the scene for sex education lessons in Year 6/P7.

● Remind children that although taking and collecting birds' eggs used to be a popular hobby, it is now illegal (unless specially licensed).

Assessment of learning outcomes

a Involvement in introduction and the Help sheet.

b Workbook page.

c Extend sheet.

Review

RESOURCES AND SETTING UP

● Adjust seating arrangements to test conditions.

a **b** Workbook pages 1 and 2.

C Extend sheet.

ACTIVITIES

Ask the children to complete the Workbook pages. Those who finish can use school resources to help them meet the challenges on the Extend sheet.

WATCHPOINTS

● Remind the children that they can also complete their own checklist about the unit when they have time. The checklist can be found at the end of the material for this unit in the photocopiable resources.

UNIT 2 Lesson 12 — Workbook 1

Stanley Thornes PRIMARY · SCIENCE

1 What happens in our bodies when we take a rest?
Example: This is when our body repairs itself / the tissues

2 What is taken from the air that goes into our lungs and helps to keep us alive? oxygen

3 Name one ingredient in each of these foods that is good for us.

potatoes
(Example answers)
starch / carbohydrate

carrot
vitamin A

milk
protein / fat / calcium
vitamins A and D

4 Label these parts of the human digestive system.

stomach
small intestine
large intestine

68

© 1997 Wendy Clemson & David Clemson. May be copied for use in purchasing school only.

UNIT 2 Lesson 12 — Workbook 2

Stanley Thornes PRIMARY · SCIENCE

5 Why do we need to wash our bodies? To keep clean / wash away bacteria (small organisms) that can cause infection / disease

6 What can happen to someone who misuses drugs? List three things:
(i) illness / accident
(ii) addiction / crime to feed habit
(iii) death / reduced life expectancy / poor quality of life

7 What is missing?
Humans have lungs and breathe air around them. Fish have gills and breath air that is in the water around them.

8 Why are plants difficult to digest? Because the parts of the plant (tiny cells) have 'walls' / covering made of cellulose which is difficult to break through.

9 What do rabbits do to help digestion? They eat vegetation which passes through their digestive system. They then eat the pellets and the food goes through the system again.

10 What job do soldier ants do? protect the ant colony

11 Ants live in colonies. Name two other insects that live like this.
(i) wasps / bees   (ii) termites

12 Name an amphibian, a reptile and an insect which lay eggs.
amphibian frog / toad / newt
reptile snake
insect moth / beetle

These could be any of the many creatures the children know – these are examples only

69

© 1997 Wendy Clemson & David Clemson. May be copied for use in purchasing school only.

OUTCOMES

EXPECTED ANSWERS

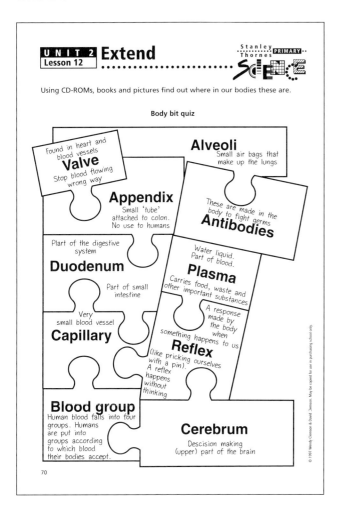

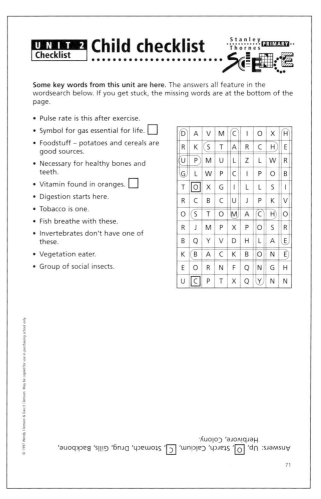

ABOUT THIS UNIT

The children are now ready to enlarge their knowledge of universal forces. The unit begins with a consideration of magnetic force, which the children will not have studied since Year 3/P4. The lessons that follow introduce electrical symbols for common apparatus they are using in the circuits they make. Lessons 4 and 5 allow the children to work on the link between 'mass' and 'weight' and what gravity is.

In lesson 5, their experiment with springs should help them to understand how a Newton meter works. There is then a discussion of what friction is and a chance to detect it experimentally. Forces at work in flight are discussed and the children have the opportunity to design, make and modify paper aeroplanes. Lessons 10 and 11 introduce the important forces at work in floating.

SPECIAL RESOURCES AND ADVANCED PLANNING

Lesson 1
For each work group two bar magnets, a clamp and stand and sling to support a freely swinging magnet are required.

Lesson 2 and 3
Circuit making apparatus is vital here.

Lesson 4
Collections of items of similar material or shape, but different sizes, including, for example, Plasticine blobs, and balls and pebbles are important for the discussion about gravity.

Lesson 5
Wire, cup hooks, pinboard and masses to hang from a spring should be collected for each work group here.

Lesson 6
Cooking oil and advertisements for car tyres should be available for this lesson. There should also be plastic or similar surfaces for the children to do the friction experiment.

Lesson 7
Advertisements for footwear and access to a range of surfaces including dry ground, wet ground, grass and an icy surface are important here.

Lesson 8
A toy replica airliner would be useful. The children may need hall space.

Lesson 9
Hall space may be required for trial paper plane flights.

Lesson 10
A glass tank or vivarium that can be filled with water and a variety of small items to place in the water to find out whether they float or sink are necessary.

Lesson 11
A plastic drinks bottle and Newton meter are among the resources required for activity **A** here. For **b** an expert coarse fisherman or woman and some fishing floats and 'weights' are useful. A hydrometer is required for activity **C**.

BOOK AND MULTIMEDIA SEARCH

Magnets
Electrical circuits
Space travel, astronauts, spacecraft and 'zero g'

Solar system
History of flight and aircraft
Floating and sinking

UNIT MAP

Lesson 1
A Observe magnetic repulsion.
b Explore magnetic force in magnets.
c Describe examples of everyday use of magnetic force.

Lesson 2
A Know that symbols are used in drawing circuit diagrams.
b Draw simple circuit diagrams.
c Interpret circuit diagrams.

Lesson 3
A Draw pictures of circuits.
b Make circuits and draw diagrams.
c Interpret and devise circuit diagrams.

Lesson 4
A Know what gravity is.
b Know what gravity does.
c Know about some record 'g' forces.

Lesson 5
A Know what a Newton is.
b Explore what happens when a spring is stretched.
c Look for items which have stretched or compressed springs in them.

Lesson 6
A Know what friction is.
b Conduct an experiment showing friction.
c Find out about friction and tyres.

Lesson 7
A Know about friction and footwear.
b Test a collection of shoes to find out how well they 'hold' in different conditions.
c Explore the importance of friction or the lack of it in the design of sportswear.

Lesson 8
A Know how things fly.
b Make and test a paper aeroplane.
c Evaluate an aeroplane design.

Lesson 9
A Know something about how aeroplanes are controlled in flight.
b Design and fly a paper aeroplane.
c Find out about historic aircraft.

Lesson 10
A Know what determines whether something floats.
b Make and test a model boat.
c Find out whether things float in liquids other than water.

Lesson 11
A Know what upthrust is.
b Find out how fishing floats work.
c Know what a hydrometer is.

Magnets

Learning intentions

a Observe magnetic repulsion.

b Explore magnetic force in magnets.

c Describe examples of everyday use of magnetic force.

Vocabulary

Attraction, effects, magnet, pole, repulsion

Lesson pattern

Whole class demonstration, practical work in groups and Workbook page, Extend sheet

RESOURCES AND SETTING UP

a Work groups will need: two bar magnets, each with the poles marked, a clamp and stand and a sling so that one magnet can be allowed to swing freely.

b Workbook page. The apparatus as for **A** for each work group in the class.

c Extend sheet, Poster 3.1. Books about magnets, their effects and uses.

ACTIVITIES

INTRODUCTION

● Remind the children of the work they did in Year 3/P4 on magnetic attraction, magnetic North and compasses. Ask them to recall what materials are attracted by a magnet. Find out if anyone can remember what happens when a magnet is allowed to hang freely.

● Hang one magnet in the sling attached to the clamp and stand. Hold the other magnet close to the freely swinging magnet, pointing at first one pole and then the other towards each of the poles of the swinging magnet. Let the children observe what happens.

a The children should observe the demonstration and see what happens.

b In their work groups the children should replicate the work the teacher did in **A** and also offer the poles of the free magnet to the centre of the other magnet. They can record their results and conclusions on the Workbook page.

c Show the children Poster 3.1. The children are required to draw or write about the uses of magnetic force in industry, our homes and lives on the Extend sheet.

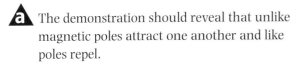

OUTCOMES

EXPECTED RESULTS

a The demonstration should reveal that unlike magnetic poles attract one another and like poles repel.

b The children's results as recorded on the work sheet should be as follows: (1) like poles repel one another; (2) unlike poles attract one another; (3) like poles repel one another; (4/5) the centre of a magnet does not seem to exert any magnetic force. The children's conclusions should include the point that like magnetic poles repel one another.

c The uses of magnets include the following:

– industry: lifting cars and scrap steel at disposal/recycling yards, electric motors,
– home: door catch, bells,
– toys: fishing games, executive toys like, magnetic rings that can be made to come to rest with one suspended above another in the air.

WATCHPOINTS

● Remind the children that magnets should be kept away from watches, videos, computers and televisions.

● If the magnetic effects do not fit expected results it may be that the magnet has become demagnetised. Try the experiment with another magnet.

Assessment of learning outcomes

a Attention to teacher demonstration.

b Workbook page.

c Extend sheet.

Circuits

Learning intentions

a Know that symbols are used in drawing circuit diagrams.

b Draw simple circuit diagrams.

c Interpret circuit diagrams.

Vocabulary

Battery, circuit, current, power source, symbol

Lesson pattern

Whole class demonstration, Help sheet, Workbook page, Extend sheet

RESOURCES AND SETTING UP

● Circuit making apparatus including: circuit wire, 4.5 or 6 volt battery, lamp, buzzer, bell, switch.

a Help sheet.

b Workbook page.

ACTIVITIES

INTRODUCTION

● Set out the circuit making apparatus where the children can see it. Remind the children of the work they have done on electric circuits in Years 3/P4 and 4/P5. Tell them that scientists draw diagrams of circuits using an agreed range of symbols to show what is wired up. These are much like symbols on a map. All scientists recognise them. Hand each child a copy of the Help sheet which shows only a few of the many circuit symbols scientists use.

● Talk through the symbols, showing the children the piece of apparatus which matches each symbol.

a Following the introduction, the children should try drawing the circuit symbols on the Help sheet.

b While the children draw in the circuit wire on the Workbook page, and then use the symbols from the Help sheet to draw a circuit diagram to match, the teacher should invent a different circuit using the classroom circuit apparatus. The children can then try drawing a circuit diagram of that circuit on the Workbook page.

c The children should look carefully at the circuit diagrams on the Extend sheet and answer the questions about them.

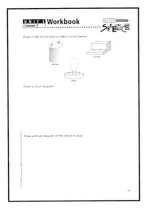

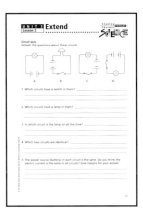

OUTCOMES

EXPECTED RESULTS

a The children should be able to replicate the circuit symbols.

....

b The circuit diagram on the Workbook page should look like this:

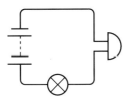

....

c The answers to the circuit quiz are as follows: (1) B, C, D; (2) A, C, D; (3) A; (4) C, D; (5) If the same lamp is in use in circuits A, C, and D, the current will be the same in these circuits. The current flowing in a circuit depends on the demands made on the power source (that is the power required for what is in the circuit).

WATCHPOINTS

● Make it clear to the children that circuit symbols have to be drawn as shown on the Help sheet in order to match the standard way of presenting them (though they many appear in any part of a circuit, and therefore may be any way up).

Assessment of learning outcomes

a Help sheet.
....
b Workbook page.
....
c Extend sheet.

Making and drawing circuits

Learning intentions

a Draw pictures of circuits.

b Make circuits and draw diagrams.

c Interpret and devise circuit diagrams.

Vocabulary

Series

Lesson pattern

Observation and Help sheet,
group work and
Workbook page,
Extend sheet

RESOURCES AND SETTING UP

a Help sheet. Circuit making apparatus including: circuit wire, 4.5 or 6 volt battery, lamp, buzzer, bell, switch.

● Using this apparatus (and other things if they are available) set up three different electrical circuits around the room.

b Workbook page. The following apparatus for each work group: circuit wire, 4.5 or 6 volt battery, 2 lamps, switch.

c Extend sheet.

ACTIVITIES

INTRODUCTION

● Invite the children to move around the room and draw pictures (not diagrams) of the three circuits set up by the teacher.

a The children should draw the classroom circuits on the Help sheet.

b The children, in their work groups, are required to make up a circuit as described on the Workbook page, and record it as a diagram. They should then place a second lamp in the circuit, observe what happens, and draw a second circuit diagram.

c The Extend sheet presents children with a number of circuit diagrams to interpret and the opportunity to draw more circuit diagrams.

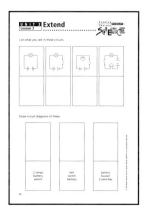

OUTCOMES

EXPECTED RESULTS

a The circuit drawings should match the circuits on view in the classroom.

b The circuit diagrams on the Workbook page should look as follows:

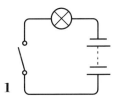 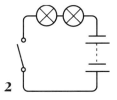

When two lamps are placed in the circuit they look dimmer than the single lamp in the same circuit.

c The answers on the Extend sheet should look as follows:

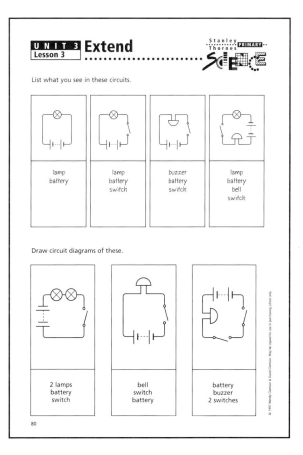

Assessment of learning outcomes

a Help sheet.

b Workbook page.

c Extend sheet.

Gravity

Learning intentions

a Know what gravity is.

b Know what gravity does.

c Know about some record 'g' forces.

Vocabulary

Acceleration, force, gravity, matter, pull

Lesson pattern

Whole class and demonstration, Workbook page, Extend sheet

RESOURCES AND SETTING UP

- Pictures of astronauts on the Moon, space walking, or moving about a spacecraft.

- Picture of the planets of the solar system in orbit around the Sun.

b Workbook page. A collection of items that are similar but of varying sizes, for example: two blobs of plasticine of different sizes, a table tennis ball, a tennis ball and a football, a pebble, a stone and a rock.

c Extend sheet. Books with information about 'g' and 'g' records (for example, *The Guinness Book of Records*).

ACTIVITIES

INTRODUCTION

- Ask the children what they know about gravity. Show the children the pictures of astronauts in space to stimulate further discussion. They may know the effects of reduced gravitational force. Ensure that the children know the following:

  - gravity is a force.
  - gravity is a force which exists between lumps of matter.
  - because the Earth's pull on us is so much greater than the pull we exert on the Earth it is the Earth's pull that keeps us here.

- Then show the children the picture of the solar system. Point out that it is the Sun's pull of gravity, which is greater than that of the planets because of its mass, which keeps all the planets in the solar system in their orbits.

a The children should participate in the introductory discussion.

b Assemble the collection of objects of different sizes. Set each range out in front of the children in turn. For example, if you have three balls of different sizes, set these down and ask the children to imagine dropping them from a high place, like a roof or several floors up in a high building. Ask the children:

- what will happen to the balls? Why do they fall to the ground?
- will the balls reach the ground in different times? If so why do they think so?

The point to make to the children is that the balls fall to the ground under the same force (that of gravity) and should reach the ground at the same time. Gravity ('g') is a measure of acceleration. Do the same actions with the other items in the collection. The children can record what they have learned in the discussion on the Workbook page.

c The children should look in encyclopaedias, etc., for information about 'g' forces to add to that on the Extend sheet.

OUTCOMES

EXPECTED RESULTS

a It is expected that the children will know something about gravity and be able to join the discussion.

b The children's answers should include the following points:

- gravity is a force.
- Isaac Newton is said to have understood the force of gravity when an apple fell on his head.
- gravity is a pull force that keeps us on the Earth.
- gravity is a pull force that occurs between lumps of matter.
- our Earth orbits the Sun because it is held by the Sun's gravity.
- when we drop things they fall to the ground because they are pulled by gravity.
- gravity is a constant force in a particular location.

c The answers here will depend on the sources the children access.

WATCHPOINTS

⚠ Warn the children of the dangers of dropping things from a height and that they should on no account try this experiment out themselves unsupervised.

● The force of gravity does vary slightly from one location on Earth to another.

● The material on the Extend sheet is taken from *The Guinness Book of Records* and is reproduced by permission of the copyright holders, Guinness Publishing Ltd.

Assessment of learning outcomes

a Participation in introductory discussion/Workbook page.

b Workbook page.

c Extend sheet.

Springs

Learning intentions

 a Know what a Newton is.

b Explore what happens when a spring is stretched.

c Look for items which have stretched or compressed springs in them.

Vocabulary

Elastic, Newton, spring, stretch, suspended

Lesson pattern

Whole class, group work and Workbook page, Extend sheet.

RESOURCES AND SETTING UP

a Help sheet.

b Workbook page. For each work group in the class: wire that is easily bendable and reasonably strong, pencil, cup hooks and pin board (or other means of securing the cup hook so that the spring the children make can be suspended from it), paper, rulers, masses (all of the same size) that can be attached to the spring.

c Extend sheet. Educational and other catalogues for a variety of goods.

ACTIVITIES

INTRODUCTION

● Remind the children of the discussion about gravity conducted in lesson 4, and that gravity is a constant. It is called 'g'. Tell the children that everything on Earth is subject to 'g' and so when we weigh things the force 'g' is pulling on what we are putting on the scales. It is also pulling on the scales themselves, so what we measure is not weight but mass. The weight of something is a measure of the Earth's pull on it multiplied by its mass, and we measure this in Newtons. This lesson is to show how we can create a tool to measure Newtons.

a The children should listen to the introduction and complete the Help sheet.

b Ask the children, in their work groups to create a spring as shown on the Workbook page and suspend it as shown. They should then add the masses in turn to the spring, marking in the length of the spring at the start and its stretched lengths and recording these and the difference between these two measures on the Workbook page.

c The children should look through the catalogues and use their own knowledge to find some items which have springs in them. They can draw some on the Extend sheet.

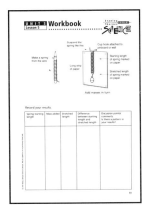

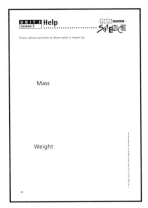

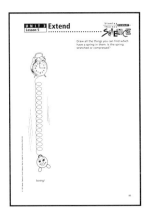

OUTCOMES

EXPECTED RESULTS

a The children should record the ideas about mass and 'weight' which are covered in the introduction above.

b The children's results should show that there is a direct relationship between the amount of stretch in the spring and the mass placed on it.

c These will depend on the items the children find, but could include, for example, toys that dangle and bounce, clockwork toys where a spring inside is wound tight and released, and desk lamps.

WATCHPOINTS

⚠ By using easily bendable wire and small masses you will avoid any danger of heavy masses falling onto tender feet.

● Ask the children to be careful not to put so many masses on the spring that it fails to return to its start length. It has then passed its elastic limit.

● A Newton meter contains a spring and a scale calibrated in Newtons. The pull on the spring can be measured and is the pull of gravity times mass. It therefore uses the principle the children demonstrate in this lesson.

Assessment of learning outcomes

 Help sheet.

 Workbook page.

 Extend sheet.

Friction

Learning intentions

a Know what friction is.

b Conduct an experiment showing friction.

c Find out about friction and tyres.

Vocabulary

Force, friction

Lesson pattern

Whole class demonstration, group work and Workbook page, Extend sheet

RESOURCES AND SETTING UP

a Help sheet. A wooden block or box, a smooth surface.

b Workbook page. Each work group will need: pencils, rubbers, water, cooking oil, a smooth surface.

c Extend sheet. Advertisements for car tyres. If there is sufficient advertising material about tyres, mount a display for the children to look at. This may include a bicycle tyre and tread patterns made with mud or paint.

ACTIVITIES

INTRODUCTION

● Place the wooden block on a smooth surface and give it a push. It should move while you push and then stop. Ask the children to explain what has happened. The force of the push moves the box. What stops the box is another force acting between the box and the surface on which it is placed. This force is acting in the opposite direction to the push and is called friction. Discuss what the children know about friction. Invite the children to complete the Help sheet.

a Following the introductory demonstration the children should complete the Help sheet, demonstrating that they recognise frictional forces.

b In their work groups ask the children to conduct the experiment described on the Workbook page making a full record of what they did.

c The children should consult the advertising material about tyres and write notes on the Extend sheet.

OUTCOMES

EXPECTED RESULTS

a The children should demonstrate on the Help sheet that they know what friction is and where it is operating.

b The record of the experiment should show that the rubber 'holds' best (i.e. there is most friction) when the surface is dry. A wet surface reduces friction somewhat and an oily surface is very slippery. The implications are that drivers of vehicles with rubber tyres should take extra care in wet conditions, or when something has been spilled on the road.

c The children should find there are claims about no skidding, 'road-holding', 'unique tread' and so on, demonstrating that the manufacturers are selling their products based on the presence of friction between tyre and road, thus preventing skidding.

WATCHPOINTS

● Remind the children that they should inspect the tread of their own bicycle tyres regularly, as a 'bald' tyre will not grip and they may skid.

Assessment of learning outcomes

a Help sheet.

b Workbook page.

c Extend sheet.

Friction and footwear

Learning intentions

a Know about friction and footwear.

b Test a collection of shoes to find out how well they 'hold' in different conditions.

c Explore the importance of friction or the lack of it in the design of sportswear.

Vocabulary

Friction, grip

Lesson pattern

Whole class, group work and Workbook page, Extend sheet

RESOURCES AND SETTING UP

a Advertisements for trainers and other footwear including walking and climbing boots.

b Workbook page. Shoes, boots, trainers and other footwear. Each work group will need five single samples. There may be one or two kinds of footwear amongst what each group is wearing and these can be used. Other kinds of footwear, e.g. plimsolls, wellingtons, flip flops or jelly shoes, need to be collected for use too. Access to dry ground, wet ground, grass, and if possible an icy surface.

c Extend sheet. Advertisements for sportswear.

ACTIVITIES

INTRODUCTION

● Talk to the children about the importance of having friction between the ground and the soles of our shoes. Ask them for examples of kinds of footwear which offer a good grip. Hold up the advertising material about footwear to provoke discussion.

a The children should join in the initial discussion.

b In their work groups the children should carry through the investigation set out on the Workbook page.

c Those children who complete the investigation can find out about friction considerations in sportswear design.

OUTCOMES

EXPECTED RESULTS

a The widespread wearing of sports shoes at all times may mean the children are well-informed about shoe design and friction.

b The results of the investigations will depend on the exact examples used and the conditions to which they are subject.

c Facts about sportswear the children may uncover include the following:

- swimwear has been designed which enables the swimmer to exceed previous best swimming speeds,
- football boots can have a contact patch on the toe section, so that good contact is made with the ball.

WATCHPOINTS

⚠ For health and safety reasons the children should not be wearing the shoes when they undertake the tests in the **b** activity.

Assessment of learning outcomes

a Participation in whole class discussion.

b Conduct of the experiment and Workbook page.

c Extend sheet.

Flight

Learning intentions

 a Know how it is that things fly.

 b Make and test a paper aeroplane.

 c Evaluate an aeroplane design.

Vocabulary

Drag, flight, gravity, lift, thrust, trial, 'weight'

Lesson pattern

Whole class, demonstration and Help sheet, practical work and Workbook page, Extend sheet

RESOURCES AND SETTING UP

 a Poster 3.8, Help sheet. Each work group will need: A4 paper suitable for making paper aeroplanes, toy aeroplane (a replica of an airliner would be ideal – it should be one with wings with a curved upper surface).

b Help sheet 2, Workbook page. It may be appropriate to arrange for the children to use the hall for their flight trials. Each child will need: A4 paper, paper clips, some Plasticine.

c Extend sheet.

ACTIVITIES

INTRODUCTION

● Show the children Poster 3.8. Explain the following important things that the children need to know to understand about flight:

– flight takes place in air.
– when air moves faster its pressure drops. Aeroplane wings provide lift because they have a curved upper surface. When the plane is taxiing for take off, the air rushes over and under the wings. The air has further to go over the wing and so moves faster. Its pressure drops. The pressure above is less than below the wing – so the plane lifts off.

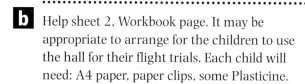
air flows faster | lower air pressure
air flows slower | greater air pressure

 a Demonstrate to the children some of the forces of thrust, drag, lift and gravity which are at work when an aeroplane is in the air. The principles can be shown as follows.

– **Lift** Make two paper aeroplanes, one as on the Help sheet and the other wingless as shown here:

Launch both aeroplanes: the one with wings should 'fly'. Ask the children why that is. In fact, the air underneath the wings exerts pressure on the plane. This pressure is lift. (This does not exactly replicate the lift explained in the introduction.)
– **Gravity** and 'weight' – remind the children of their work in lessons 4 and 5 about gravity. This force pulls the plane to earth.
– **Thrust** This is the force of the engine power pushing the plane forward.
– **Drag** This is the air resistance which acts to slow the plane in the air. Aeroplanes are built in special shapes to minimise drag.

Hand out copies of Help sheet 1 and discuss the forces at work.

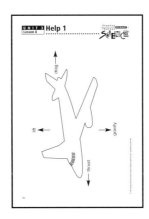

b The children should make a paper aeroplane using the instructions on Help sheet 2. They should then work with a partner in conducting the experiment on the Workbook page. Each child should have the chance to throw five times, measure these distances and then modify their plane before conducting the experiment again.

c The children should reflect on the experiment they conducted in **b** and write about changes they would make to the design to improve it.

OUTCOMES

EXPECTED RESULTS

a The children should understand how it is that heavy planes can get off the ground and the forces at work on planes.

b This experiment should enable children to conduct a fair test and compare sets of results, and also consolidate some of what they have learned about flight.

c This activity should give children experience of experimental evaluation.

WATCHPOINTS

● Ask the children to put their names on their aeroplanes and keep them for the next session.

⚠ Ensure that when the children test their aeroplanes there is no risk of a plane being thrown at, or flying into, the face of another child.

Assessment of learning outcomes

a Involvement in introduction and demonstration.

b Workbook page.

c Extend sheet.

Flight 2

Learning intentions

a Know something about how aeroplanes are controlled in flight.

b Design and fly a paper aeroplane.

c Find out about historic aircraft.

Vocabulary

Ailerons, elevators, rudder, wing flaps

Lesson pattern

Whole class, practical work and Workbook page, Extend sheet

RESOURCES AND SETTING UP

a Help sheet.

b Workbook page. It may be appropriate to arrange for the children to use the hall for their flight trials. Children will need: A4 paper for aeroplane making, scissors, measuring tapes.

c Extend sheet, Poster 3.8. Books about the history of flight.

ACTIVITIES

INTRODUCTION

● Hand out copies of the Help sheet. Talk through the ways a pilot controls an aeroplane.

a The children should scrutinise the Help sheet and discuss it in the introductory part of the lesson.

b Invite the children to draw a paper aeroplane design on the Workbook page. They can then make up their design and test it, working in pairs, so that they can help one another in measuring the distances and recording their results over trials. They can also compare this aeroplane with the model they made in Lesson 8.

c Using research resources the children should find out about the historic aircraft shown on the Extend sheet. Poster 3.8 will be helpful here.

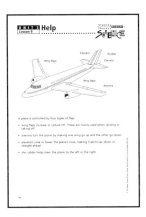
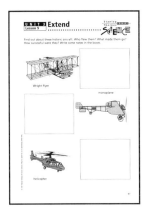

OUTCOMES

EXPECTED RESULTS

a The diagram on the Help sheet should give the children some understanding about how an aeroplane is controlled in the air.

b The children should be able to conduct the experiment successfully, demonstrating that they know about 'trial and improvement' and make modifications in the light of what they know about flight, which may make their paper plane fly better.

c Results will depend on the resources the children use. Here is some information about the images on the Extend sheet. If the children cannot find these they can research other pioneering aircraft:

- the Wright flyer: built by Americans Orville and Wilbur Wright in 1903, it had a petrol engine.
- the monoplane: in 1909 the Frenchman Blériot flew in this across the English Channel.
- the helicopter: early helicopters had two blades which turned in opposite directions. A single rotor helicopter was made in the USA by Russian born Igor Sikorsky in 1939.

WATCHPOINTS

⚠ Ensure that when the children test their aeroplanes there is no risk of a plane being thrown at, or flying into, the face of another child.

Assessment of learning outcomes

a Participation in the introduction.

b Workbook page and conduct of the experiment.

c Extend sheet.

Floating

Learning intentions

a Know what determines whether something floats.

b Make and test a model boat.

c Find out whether things float in liquids other than water.

Vocabulary

Float, sink

Lesson pattern

Whole class demonstration, group work and Workbook page, practical work and Extend sheet

---

RESOURCES AND SETTING UP

 Work groups will need:

a clear glass tank of water, things to demonstrate floating and sinking, including Plasticine, cooking foil, balsa wood, cork, pebble and other small items. It may prove possible to include the items the children worked with in Year 4/P5 Unit 3, Lesson 8. They are as follows: button, cotton reel, stick, paper clip, plastic cup, sponge, soap, marble.

b Workbook page. The following are required for each work group in the class: access to a tank of water, empty fast food containers made of polystyrene or foil, Plasticine, paper, building blocks (Lego or similar blocks are ideal).

c Extend sheet. Work groups will need: a tank of water as used in **b**, a tank containing cooking oil, a tank containing salt water, a toy boat or the best of the model boats used in **b**.

ACTIVITIES

INTRODUCTION

● Remind the children of the work they did in Year 4/P5. Ask the children to predict which things might float when dropped into the tank of water. Discuss their reasons for these predictions.

 While the children look on, ask volunteers to drop each of the items in turn into the tank of water. The children may say 'heavy things sink'. Indicate that while a ball of Plasticine sinks, if it is made into a boat/dish shape it will float. Check that the children understand that whether something floats actually depends on its density, i.e. its mass divided by its volume (the space it takes up) compared with that of water. The ball of Plasticine will sink because it is denser than the water in the tank. When its shape is boat-like, the density of the Plasticine plus that of the air in the 'boat' is less than that of water and so it floats.

b Invite the children to get into their work groups and each make a boat from the materials provided. They should try to produce a polystyrene boat, a foil boat, a plasticine boat and a paper boat. They should then follow the Workbook page in testing out the boats and record their results.

c The children should be allowed to try floating a model boat in a tank of fresh water, salt water and then cooking oil and note the difference in the way the boat sits in the liquid. They can then try to connect their findings with the information about the Plimsoll line.

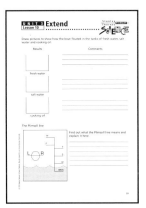

OUTCOMES

EXPECTED RESULTS

a It is expected that the children will be able to predict that things like a cork or wooden block will float, whereas a ball of Plasticine will not.

b The children should be able to carry through the experiment. The 'best' of their boats will depend on their constituents and design.

c The boat should sit higher in the salt water than in fresh water, and higher still in the cooking oil. This indicates the differences in density in different liquids. The Plimsoll line tells the captain the maximum safe cargo for fresh and salt water travel.

WATCHPOINTS

● Ensure the children wash their hands with soap and water to remove any cooking oil they may pick up.

Assessment of learning outcomes

a Participation in the introduction and demonstration.

b Workbook page.

c Extend sheet.

Buoyancy

Learning intentions

a Know what upthrust is.

b Find out how fishing floats work.

c Know what a hydrometer is.

Vocabulary

Buoyancy, density, upthrust

Lesson pattern

Whole class demonstration and Help sheet, demonstration and Workbook page, Extend sheet

---

RESOURCES AND SETTING UP

a Help sheet. A large stone, a tank of water, string, strong elastic band or length of elastic, Newton meter.

b Workbook page. If a parent or colleague is a coarse fisherman or woman and they have time to talk to the children that would be helpful here.

Fishing floats and weights, a tank of water.

c Extend sheet. Hydrometer or information about a hydrometer, sample liquids in beakers (include water, milk, golden syrup and cough syrup).

ACTIVITIES

INTRODUCTION

● Tell the children that this lesson is to be about the forces involved in floating and sinking. Pose these puzzles to the children. Ask the children why it is that when in a swimming pool you can stand in shallow water and keep your feet on the bottom, but as the water gets deeper your feet start to come off the bottom? Why, also is it easier to float if you take a deep breath first? See what the children say and tell them that they will return to these puzzles during the lesson.

 a While all the children look on, tie a piece of thread around a large stone or piece of brick. Attach a stout elastic band to the string and gently lift the stone off the table just a little. Ask the children to observe the length of the band when stretched. If a Newton meter is available attach this to the string and let the children read off the weight of the stone. Then gently place the stone in a tank of water so that it lies on the bottom. Try lifting the stone again. Ask the children to observe the stretched rubber band. Attach the Newton meter to the string again and let the children take another reading. Discuss what the children observe. Ask them to record what has happened on the Help sheet.

b Show the children a range of fishing floats. Point out that the fisherman wants to detect a 'bite' by means of the float, so the float's position in the water is very important. Floats can be weighted to alter the amount that is above water. Show the children how this is done. They can make a record of their learning on the Workbook page.

c If a hydrometer is available, the children should suspend it in the sample liquids in turn, and see what happens. Outcomes can be recorded on the Extend sheet. If a hydrometer is not available the children should look for and copy a picture of one on the Extend sheet.

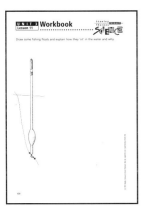

OUTCOMES

EXPECTED RESULTS

a The rubber band attached to the stone should not stretch as much when the stone is in water. The weight of the stone will appear to be less in the water. The water is pushing (exerting pressure) on the stone upwards. This upward force is called upthrust. The upthrust is the difference between what the stone weighed in air and what it weighs in the water. Upthrust increases as more water is displaced, i.e. the stone sinks through the surface of the water. This explains why our feet come off the bottom of a pool as the water gets deeper. As we sink further into the water, more water is displaced and upthrust increases to lift our feet off the bottom of the pool.

b Remind the children of work done in Lesson 10, and tell them that the weighting of the floats alters their density relative to the water. On the Workbook page the children can do some drawings to explain what they have learned. In water people float better with more air in their lungs because this reduces their density (body plus air in lungs) relative to that of the water.

c Hydrometer readings will depend on the actual sample liquids used.

WATCHPOINTS

● Carefully try out the experiment with the stone before doing it in front of the children, in order to check that the rubber band is strong enough.

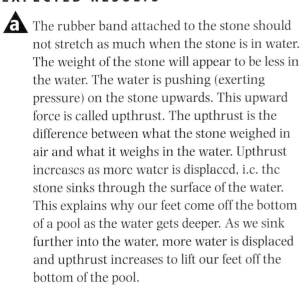

Assessment of learning outcomes

a Help sheet.

b Workbook page.

c Extend sheet.

Review

RESOURCES AND SETTING UP

● Adjust seating arrangements to test conditions.

a **b** Workbook pages 1 and 2.

c Extend sheet.

ACTIVITIES

Ask the children to complete the Workbook pages. Those who finish can respond to the questions about forces involved in a tug of war on the Extend sheet.

WATCHPOINTS

● Remind the children that they can also complete their own checklist about the unit when they have time. The checklist can be found at the end of the material for this unit in the photocopiable resources.

OUTCOMES

EXPECTED ANSWERS

- Work on the Extend sheet may yield some of the following ideas:

  - forces at work include the pull forces of the teams in both directions.
  - there is friction between their feet and the ground and their hands and the rope.
  - one team may improve their chances of winning by (for example) wearing footwear allowing more friction, wearing gloves to improve grip, adding to the total mass of the team by having heavier people in the team.

UNIT 3 Lesson 12 — Workbook 1

Stanley Thornes PRIMARY SCIENCE

1 What happens when magnets are placed like this?

They repel one another

2 What do these electrical symbols mean?

battery   switch   lamp

3 What happens when a second lamp is put into a circuit with one lamp already in it?

The lamps get dimmer

4 What force stops us falling off the Earth?   gravity

5 Why do astronauts weigh less in space? There is less / zero 'g' or gravity

6 What can you say about the distance a spring stretches when a mass is hung on it? There is a direct link between 'amount of stretch' and mass hung on the spring.

© 1997 Wendy Clemson & David Clemson. May be copied for use in purchasing school only.

103

UNIT 3 Lesson 12 — Workbook 2

Stanley Thornes PRIMARY SCIENCE

7 What would happen if there was no friction between your shoes and the ground?

You would be unable to stand / walk and would continually slip over

8 If we cut through an aeroplane wing it is shaped like this. Why is it this shape?

To give the plane 'lift' using air pressure

9 These are all made of Plasticine.

Tick any you think will float.

10 What appears to happen when a stone is hung in water?

It appears to weigh less

Why? Because of the upthrust of the water

© 1997 Wendy Clemson & David Clemson. May be copied for use in purchasing school only.

101

ABOUT THIS UNIT

Animal classification and keys are the starting point for work in this unit. Some of the main groupings in classification can now be mastered and then applied in the lessons that follow where plant families and keys are studied. Children working at Key Stage 2 are required to become familiar with animal adaptation and habitat. To extend their knowledge, two locations, the sea-shore and the pond, have been selected. In these settings there are a range of opportunities to look at plant and animal life. Concern for the environment and pollution is currently an issue which frequently features in newspaper headlines. To begin to help the children understand these stories, litter has been chosen as the first pollutant, because it is within children's own experience and they themselves can do something about it. Information about acid rain also features in this part of the Unit for it will link with the work the children have done in Unit 1 on acids and indicators. The final part of the Unit enables children to identify and explore food chains and predator/prey relationships and looks at human measures to protect the environment.

SPECIAL RESOURCES AND ADVANCED PLANNING

Lesson 3
Four sample flowering plants are necessary for the children to examine. 'Wild' plants that are in flower would be ideal.

Lesson 4
Sample plants or leaves are required.

Lesson 7
A range of items that are often found littering the environment would be helpful in this lesson.

Lesson 8
For activity ❻ litmus paper or universal indicator is required along with rain water samples from a variety of locations.

Lesson 11
A visiting expert, who can talk about measures being taken to enhance environmental protection, should be sought for this lesson.

BOOK AND MULTIMEDIA SEARCH

Animals
Animal classification
Plants
Plant classification

Life on the sea-shore
Pond life
Acid rain

UNIT MAP

Lesson 1
A Know some groupings in animal classification.
b Identify some animal groupings.
c Search and find the groups to which named animals belong.

Lesson 2
A Understand why we use animal keys.
b Read and interpret a key classifying animals.
c Devise a key to name some creatures.

Lesson 3
A Name a number of plant species.
b Find out the groups to which sample plants belong.
c Investigate a plant family.

Lesson 4
A Know how keys can be applied to plants.
b Compare leaves and suggest features to aid identification.
c Devise a key.

Lesson 5
A Know some of the plants and animals found on the sea-shore.
b Give reasons why some living things are found in this habitat.
c Identify a good source of information about sea-shore life.

Lesson 6
A Know some of the plants and animals found in or around a pond.
b Give reasons why some living things are found in this habitat.
c Find out about the life histories of the grasshopper and mosquito.

Lesson 7
A Know why litter is an environmental hazard.
b Explore what can be done to reduce litter.
c Know what biodegradable means.

Lesson 8
A Know what acid rain is.
b Know what acid rain does.
c Test rain for acidity.

Lesson 9
A Know what the words predator and prey mean.
b Identify some predators and prey.
c Find out about animal population controls.

Lesson 10
A Know some of the vocabulary associated with food chains.
b Construct some food chains.
c Research and record some food chains.

Lesson 11
A Know why animals and plants are in danger.
b Know about the work of an environmental group.
c Think about the protection of the local environment.

Animal groups

Learning intentions

 Know some groupings in animal classification.

 Identify some animal groupings.

c Search and find the groups to which named animals belong.

Vocabulary

Class, classification, genera, genus, kingdom, order, species

Lesson pattern

Whole class, group work and research, Workbook page, research and Extend sheet

RESOURCES AND SETTING UP

● Books and other resources about classifying animals. All children will need access to these, so pages from relevant books could be photocopied before the lesson.

 Help sheet.

 Workbook page.

 Extend sheet.

ACTIVITIES

INTRODUCTION

● Remind the children of the work they did in Year 3/P4, Unit 1 and Year 4/P5, Unit 2 on animal groupings. See if they can remember groups of vertebrates or invertebrates. Tell the children that animals are put into groups so that they can be named and identified easily. The smallest important group they are put into is the species. A species comprises all animals that can have young who in their turn are able to have young.

a The children should take part in the introductory discussion. Then hand out copies of the Help sheet and work through it with the children. Explain that the 'small' group, the species, is included in a larger group, and so on until the group including all animals (the animal kingdom) is reached. There are lots of groupings. The Help sheet mentions some of them.

b Divide the class into work groups and allocate, 'fish', 'birds' or 'mammals' to each group so that all three are represented. Invite the children to find an 'order' within the class they are studying, and find examples of groups of creatures which fit in this order. Their work can be recorded on the Workbook page.

c Using the resources available in the classroom the children are required to find out what groups of animals the sting ray, koala, wild cat and greylag goose belong to.

OUTCOMES

EXPECTED RESULTS

a Following the introduction the children should know some of the groups to which animals belong.

b Outcomes will depend on the order chosen by the children, see Watchpoints.

c The groupings the children may find are as follows:

sting ray	class Chondrichthyes (fish with cartilage skeleton)
	family Dasyatidae
	Dasyatis pastinaca
koala	class Mammalia
	family Phalangeridae
	Phascolarctos cinereus
wild cat	class Mammalia
	family Felidae
	Felis sylvestris
greylag goose	class Aves
	family Anatidae
	Anser anser

WATCHPOINTS

- Within species there are 'varieties' (for example, breeds of dog) but varieties can interbreed; species cannot. In other words, animals and plants in a species can produce fertile offspring. They all share some characteristics. Members of a species will also have in common some features of the genus, family and order to which they belong.

- A starting point for classification can be found in *Signs, Symbols and Systematics: the ASE Companion to 5–16 Science*, published by the Association for Science Education, June 1995.

Assessment of learning outcomes

a Participation in early part of the lesson and attention to the Help sheet.

b Workbook page.

c Extend sheet.

Using keys

Learning intentions

 Understand why we use animal keys.

b Read and interpret a key classifying animals.

c Devise a key to name some creatures.

Vocabulary

Characteristic, classification, classify, key

Lesson pattern

Whole class, Help sheet, Workbook page, Extend sheet

RESOURCES AND SETTING UP

- Books about animals, animal classification and the use of keys. Live specimens of small creatures, which the teacher has identified before the lesson would add to the introductory discussion, but these are not essential.

 Help sheet 1.

b Workbook page, Help sheet 2.

c Extend sheet.

ACTIVITIES

INTRODUCTION

- Remind the children of work they did in Year 4/P5, Units 2 and 4 about keys. Ask them what a key is when used to classify animals. Check that they understand that scientists use keys in order to find the name of a creature easily. If there are live creatures in the classroom, show them to the children and talk through the features or characteristics that might be important in sorting out the name of each. Try drawing a sample key on the blackboard.

 The children should look carefully at the pictures on Help sheet 1 and then answer the question.

b The children are asked to interpret the key on the Workbook page and then determine the questions they would ask in trying to name the small creatures drawn on the Workbook page. Help sheet 2 shows another way of presenting the same key.

c The children are asked to devise a key for naming three creatures portrayed on the Extend sheet.

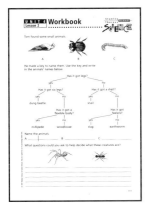  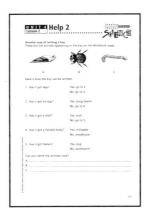 

OUTCOMES

EXPECTED RESULTS

a The answer the children give to the question about why scientists use keys should relate to ease and speed of naming creatures.

b The answers to the animal key are (A) slug, (B) dung beetle, (C) millipede. There are a variety of questions the children could ask about the other creatures including.

- Has it got legs? Has it got six legs? Has it got eight legs?
- Has it got three body parts? Has it got two body parts?
- Has it got feelers?

These specimens are a house spider and a black ant.

c The children may arrive at their own key. The questions that might arise in the key are as shown here (see also under Watchpoints):

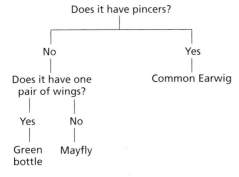

Does it have pincers?

No — Yes

Does it have one pair of wings? — Common Earwig

Yes — No

Green bottle — Mayfly

WATCHPOINTS

- If small creatures are brought into the classroom, ensure that they are kept in secure containers, away from direct sunlight, and returned to the place where they were found, as soon as is feasible after the lesson.

⚠ Ensure children wash their hands with soap and water if they handle the animals.

- The key shown in the previous column is only an example. The child may focus on other features including colours, presence of tails, size of feelers, etc. (The greenbottle and other true flies have only one pair of functional wings. The hind wings are tiny, pin-like and help in maintaining balance in flight.)

Assessment of learning outcomes

a Help sheet.

b Workbook page.

c Extend sheet.

Plants

Learning intentions

 a Name a number of plant species.

b Find out the groups to which sample plants belong.

c Investigate a plant family.

Vocabulary

Plant family, names of specific families required by the children

Lesson pattern

Whole class, Help sheet, group work and Workbook page, Extend sheet

---

RESOURCES AND SETTING UP

a Help sheet.

b Workbook page.

Books about flowering plants and their names. Field guides and other books assisting plant identification.

At least four sample plants for the children to inspect. All the children will need access to these for activity **b**. These should be in flower if possible, and 'wild' preferably so that they feature in wild flower books rather than gardening books. The plants should all come from different plant families.

It may be appropriate to set up the samples around the room so that the middle part of the lesson can be run as a workshop with the children moving around.

The teacher should check the names of the plants before the lesson.

c Extend sheet.

ACTIVITIES

INTRODUCTION

● Talk to the children about the plants they can identify and local habitats they know where there are a wide variety of plants. Remind the children of all the work they have done on plants and their names.

a The children should study the plant pictures on the Help sheet. If the flap is folded down they can test themselves on plant names and family names. If it is appropriate they can colour some of the plant pictures in the correct colours.

b In their work group the children should inspect the sample plants on display and find out the names of the families to which they belong. They should record their findings on the Workbook page.

c The children should take any plant family they like (it may be one from the Help sheet, or from among those which are displayed in the classroom, or a new family). They are required to create a small book using the Extend sheet.

OUTCOMES

EXPECTED RESULTS

a It is expected that the children will recognise some of the plant names, learn some more, and learn some family names.

b The families identified will depend on the actual examples on display in class.

c The booklets the children produce should provide a resource for the whole class to use.

WATCHPOINTS

● This lesson can be adapted to fit in with local conditions. If appropriate a new Help sheet can be created with pictures of 15 plants common in the area around the school. The sample plants brought into the classroom can also match local flora.

⚠ Ensure children wash their hands with soap and water after handling plants.

Assessment of learning outcomes

a Observation of the children using the Help sheet.

b Workbook page.

c Extend sheet.

Plant keys

Learning intentions

a Know how keys can be applied to plants.

b Compare leaves and suggest features to aid identification.

c Devise a key.

Vocabulary

Characteristics, compound, features, identify, key, leaf, leaflet, simple, tooth

Lesson pattern

Whole class, Workbook page, Extend sheet

RESOURCES AND SETTING UP

● Poster 4.4.

a Several sample plants or leaves to show the children.

b Workbook page.

c Extend sheet.

ACTIVITIES

INTRODUCTION

● Show the children Poster 4.4 and the selection of leaves or plants in the collection. Explain that scientists use plant keys in much the same way as animal keys in identifying and naming plants. The children will have been reminded in the last lesson that plants belong to families, and that members of a family are alike in some ways. Using observation of the leaves on the plants or the leaves in the collection, identify some features which distinguish one leaf from another. Questions may include:

– is it a simple leaf (with one part only)?
– does it have leaflets (small leaves all attached to a single stalk)?
– does the leaf have teeth?
– are the teeth large or small?

Other features the children may wish to add include shape, colours, appearance (glossy or dull), from a deciduous or evergreen tree.

a The children should observe the leaves and take part in the introduction to the lesson.

b Using the Workbook page the children should look carefully at the example leaves displayed and decide, for each group of three, which they think go together and which is the odd one out. They can then reflect on the question they may ask in each case, to determine the odd one out.

c The children should try devising a key for the leaves shown on the Extend sheet.

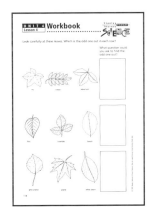

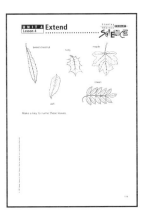

OUTCOMES

EXPECTED RESULTS

a It is expected that the children should now understand what plant and animal keys are for.

b The answers will depend on the children's own judgement. Here is an example set of answers:

- Row 1 – the ivy because it is a simple leaf and the others have leaflets; the question is 'Is the leaf simple?'
- Row 2 – the bramble because it has leaflets while the others are simple (or the bramble because the leaf has small teeth); the question could be 'Is the leaf simple/compound?' or 'Has the leaf got small teeth?'
- Row 3 – the white beam because it has small teeth while the others have large teeth (or an indication that the white beam differs in shape from the other two examples, and they are more alike); the question could be 'Does the leaf have small teeth?' or 'Is the leaf shaped like an elongated oval?'

c The children may choose a variety of features to place in their key. One example is shown here.

WATCHPOINTS

⚠ Be careful as some plants can irritate the skin. Wash hands with soap and water after handling plants.

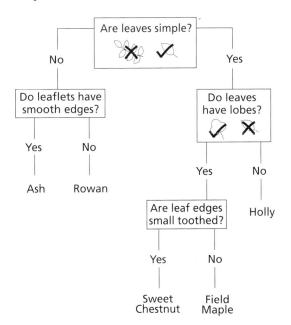

Assessment of learning outcomes

a Participation in the introduction to the lesson.

b Workbook page.

c Extend sheet.

UNIT 4
Living things in their environment
LESSON 5

Sea-shore life

Learning intentions

a Know some of the plants and animals found on the sea-shore.

b Give reasons why some living things are found in this habitat.

c Identify a good source of information about sea-shore life. 2/s/a,b

Vocabulary

Adaptation, cliff, dune, features, habitat, life style, rock pool, species, structure, tide line

Lesson pattern

Whole class and Help sheet, Workbook page, Extend sheet

RESOURCES AND SETTING UP

a Help sheet.

b Help sheet, Workbook page.

c Extend sheet. Books about animal and plant life on and near the sea-shore.

ACTIVITIES

INTRODUCTION

● Talk about the children's own experiences when walking or holidaying on the sea-shore. Ask them what signs of life they saw there. See how many sea-shore plants and animals they can recall from their work in Year 3/P4, Unit 1 and from their own experiences. Talk to the children about why some of these creatures are found there. For example:

– water dwellers need or tolerate salt water.
– crustaceans have bodies protected from hurt against rocks and predators like gulls.
– some creatures need a location where food comes to them, e.g. limpets and sea anemones.
– plants are narrow leafed, low growing, and tolerant of poor soil so that they can live in windy conditions without uprooting, and can sustain growth when soil is sandy and salty.

a The children should take part in the initial discussion and then examine carefully the picture on the Help sheet.

b Using the Help sheet the children should choose some of the living things depicted there and explain on the Workbook page why they think they live on the sea-shore.

c The children should inspect some resources about sea-shore life and review one that they think is particularly good on the Extend sheet.

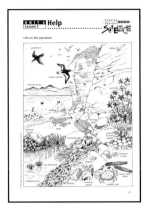

OUTCOMES

EXPECTED RESULTS

a It is expected that the children will recall or now understand that specific living things are adapted to the environment in which they live.

b The children's reasons will depend on the creatures they choose. All answers which fit the scientific facts about the creatures are acceptable.

c The children's choice of resource will depend on what is available. There are enormous numbers of books about animals, plants and habitats aimed at the junior age range. There are also impressive CD-ROMs available.

WATCHPOINTS

● The children's lists of animal and plant features which fit them for this habitat need not be exhaustive. However, it is expected that they should give salient scientific reasons why the animals and plants they have chosen live on the sea-shore.

Assessment of learning outcomes

a Attention during early part of the lesson.

b Workbook page.

c Extend sheet.

Pond life

Learning intentions

a Know some of the plants and animals found in or around a pond.

b Give reasons why some living things are found in this habitat.

c Find out about the life histories of the grasshopper and mosquito.

Vocabulary

Adaptation, banks, features, habitat, lake, life style, pond, species, structure, surface film

Lesson pattern

Whole class and Help sheet,
Workbook page,
Extend sheet

RESOURCES AND SETTING UP

a Help sheet.

b Help sheet, Workbook page.

c Extend sheet. Books about animal and plant life in and near a pond.

ACTIVITIES

INTRODUCTION

● Talk about the children's own experiences when exploring ponds. Ask them what signs of life they saw there. See how many pond plants and animals they can recall from their work in Year 3/P4, Unit 1 and from their own experiences. Talk to the children about why some of these creatures are found there, for example:

- some plants are water tolerant, or are specially adapted to growing in water.
- some insects are built so that they can stand and move on the surface film of the water.
- underwater creatures often have gills and need fresh water to survive.
- some creatures like frogs, toads and lizards require damp places and fresh water for some or all their life phases.

a The children should take part in the initial discussion and then examine carefully the picture on the Help sheet.

b Using the Help sheet the children should look carefully at some of the living things depicted there and explain what features they would expect to find in living things, on, in and around the pond. Their findings should be recorded on the Workbook page.

c The children should find out about the stages in the life history of the grasshopper and the mosquito and add the labels to the diagrams on the Extend sheet.

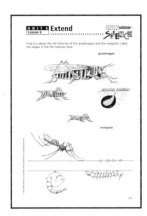

OUTCOMES

EXPECTED RESULTS

a It is expected that the children will recall or now understand that specific living things are adapted to the environment in which they live. Note that not all living things depicted on the Help sheet will necessarily be around at the same time of the year.

b All the features given by the children and borne out by observation are acceptable, for example:

– on the pond, plants need to have roots that tolerate submersion without rotting, leaves that are shiny to avoid becoming waterlogged, and that float; animals can surface swim or land on the surface film.

– in the pond, the points above about plants 'on the pond' also apply here; plants root easily, are tolerant of a variety of subsoils, grow rapidly (and therefore do not die away completely where they are eaten); underwater creatures have gills or absorb oxygen through the skin.

– around the pond, the range of plants and animals increases as they can be atmospheric air breathing; the pond provides a valuable water source for all creatures.

c The children should find labels that match those opposite.

WATCHPOINTS

● The children's lists of animal and plant features which fit them for this habitat need not be exhaustive.

● Warn children of the dangers and risks of accidents in ponds.

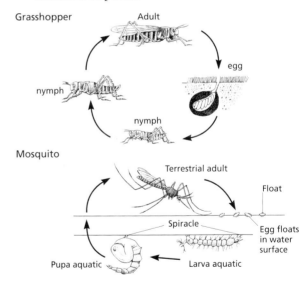

Assessment of learning outcomes

a Attention during early part of the lesson.

b Workbook page.

c Extend sheet.

Litter

Learning intentions

a Know why litter is an environmental hazard.

b Explore what can be done to reduce litter.

c Know what biodegradable means.

Vocabulary

Environmental hazard, litter, prevention

Lesson pattern

Whole class,
Workbook page,
Extend sheet

RESOURCES AND SETTING UP

● Poster 4.7.

● A variety of types of litter including some of the items depicted on the Extend sheet could be displayed prior to discussion though they are not essential.

b Workbook page.

c Extend sheet.

ACTIVITIES

INTRODUCTION

● Discuss the problem of litter with the children, and show them the poster to stimulate discussion. Check that the children understand that litter can be a health hazard to humans and animals. Animals can suffer injury when in contact with sharp edges or packaging in which they become entangled. They are also at risk of swallowing indigestible material. Rubbish can contaminate fresh and sea water and feeding grounds. Talk about what can be designated litter, the kinds of materials from which it is made, and whether the litter will change if left on or in the ground.

a The children should listen to and join in the introductory discussion.

b The children should get into work groups and decide together on a five-point action plan to eliminate litter. They can record their work on the Workbook page.

c A definition for biodegradable must be sought, and, acting on this definition, the children should decide which of the items on the Extend sheet are biodegradable. If a display has been arranged in the classroom this could prompt further discussion.

OUTCOMES

EXPECTED RESULTS

 Following the discussion the children should understand what litter is and the dangers it poses.

b The action points raised by the children may vary. Here are some suggestions:

- plenty of litter bins and regular emptying.
- signs telling people of the dangers of litter.
- less packaging by manufacturers.
- fines for litter dropping.

c Biodegradable means that an object will decompose ('rot' or break down) due to the action of micro-organisms like bacteria. The children need to know that biodegradable items are 'safe' to put in the ground for they do not remain in their present state forever, which would contaminate the ground. The following items are probably biodegradable (though actual composition really needs to be known):

- spent match, apple core, old leather shoe, paper tissue, block of wood (some of these would take a long time to be restored to ground, but they are 'natural' materials).

WATCHPOINTS

⚠ The 'litter items' put on display should be 'clean' items to represent litter and not items retrieved from outside as they may be contaminated.

Assessment of learning outcomes

a Involvement in early discussion, group work and work on the Workbook page.

b Workbook page.

c Extend sheet.

Acid rain

Learning intentions

 Know what acid rain is.

 Know what acid rain does.

 Test rain for acidity.

Vocabulary

Acid, acidity, effects, gas, neutral, pollution

Lesson pattern

Whole class and Help sheet, Workbook page, practical work and Extend sheet.

RESOURCES AND SETTING UP

a Help sheet.

b Workbook page

c Extend sheet. Books and other information sources (e.g. press cuttings) about acid rain. Litmus paper or universal indicator (the latter would be better for it gives a more sensitive indication of acidity), beakers. Labelled rain water samples from different locations. These could include a playground puddle, a garden water butt and a sample collected by the children, by leaving a container outside during a shower.

ACTIVITIES

INTRODUCTION

● Explain to the children what acid rain is. Hand out copies of the Help sheet and read through the sheet aloud. Discuss with the children what effects acid rain has and how its extent could be reduced.

a The children should listen to the introduction, and read through the Help sheet.

b Following the introduction the children should read the newspaper article on the Workbook page (along with any other newspaper cuttings which are available), and record actions they think will reduce acid rain. Some children may require help with the text and in arriving at their answers.

 The children should carefully test the rain water samples available with the litmus paper to see if any are acid. Their recordings should be made on the Extend sheet.

OUTCOMES

EXPECTED RESULTS

a The children should understand what acid rain is, following the introduction.

b The children should understand what acid rain does, following their work on the Workbook page. Acid rain can be reduced by limiting the emissions from factories and cars.

c Local rain samples should be neutral, denoted by no change to pink or blue litmus.

WATCHPOINTS

⚠ The rainwater samples should be collected by the teacher before the lesson, or by children before the lesson in locations supervised by the teacher.

● If the rain samples are acid this should be further investigated. Contact the local council to find out who is responsible for environmental monitoring.

● The material on the Workbook page is taken from the *Guardian*, 20 October 1992, 'Acid Rain: sharp showers', by Ruth Coleman, and is used by permission of the copyright holders.

Assessment of learning outcomes

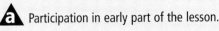

a Participation in early part of the lesson.

b Workbook page.

c Extend sheet.

Predators and prey

Learning intentions

a Know what the words predator and prey mean.

b Identify some predators and prey.

c Find out about animal population controls.

2/5/c

Vocabulary

Balance, population control, predator, prey, survival

Lesson pattern

Whole class, Workbook page, Extend sheet

RESOURCES AND SETTING UP

● Books about predators, prey and the natural control of animal populations.

b Workbook page.

c Extend page.

ACTIVITIES

INTRODUCTION

● Tell the children what the words predator and prey mean (explanations are set out on the Workbook page).

a The children should listen to definitions of predator and prey.

b The children should complete the Workbook page and should then find and list some more creatures they know to be predators and prey.

c Using resources available the children should look up how it is that animals do not die out, because they are successful in catching and eating their prey.

OUTCOMES

EXPECTED RESULTS

a The children should be able to understand what is meant by predators and prey.

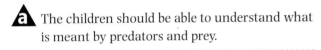

b On the Workbook page the following are the appropriate labels:

Predator	Prey
fox	rabbit
frog	fly
pike	water beetle
spider	butterfly
common long-eared bat	moth
greater spotted woodpecker	tree grub

c The examples found by the children will depend on the resources used.

Assessment of learning outcomes

a Attention to the introduction.

b Workbook page.

c Extend sheet.

Food chains

Learning intentions

a Know some of the vocabulary associated with food chains.

b Construct some food chains.

c Research and record some food chains.

2\5\d.

Vocabulary

Consumer, food chain, producer.

Lesson pattern

Whole class, Help sheet and Workbook page, research and Extend sheet

---

RESOURCES AND SETTING UP

a **b** Workbook page, Help sheet. Books about food chains, the living world and what creatures eat. Scissors, paper, glue (sufficient for the whole class).

c Extend sheet.

ACTIVITIES

INTRODUCTION

● Remind the children of the work they did on food chains in Year 4/P5, Unit 4. Ask them what a food chain is. Check that they understand that all food chains start with a plant, as plants produce their own food. All other living things are therefore dependent on plants. They are called consumers. In a food chain the supply of plants needs to be large compared with the numbers of creatures further up the chain. Many creatures have varied diets so food chains often connect with one another in complex webs. Quiz the children on the vocabulary of food chains until they fully understand it.

a The children should take part in the introductory discussion.

b The children should cut out the images on the Help sheet and stick them in the correct locations on the Workbook page, showing how the food chains are configured.

c Using appropriate research sources the children are asked to create four food chains on the Extend sheet. The first two are to start with an oak leaf and a nasturtium, and the remaining ones are to end with a cormorant and a common seal.

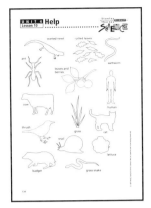

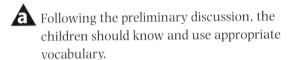

OUTCOMES

EXPECTED RESULTS

a Following the preliminary discussion, the children should know and use appropriate vocabulary.

b The food chains on the Workbook page should go as follows:

rotted leaves – earthworm – badger
leaves and berries ants – crested or warty
   newt – grass snake
grass – cattle – human
lettuce – garden snail – thrush – cat

c The food chains the children devise will depend on the sources used. However, all four should begin with a plant. If there is not time to find and record all four chains, the children could each find one chain, and then pool efforts and draw in three of the outcomes of their classmates.

WATCHPOINTS

● Food chains involve energy transfer to sustain life.

● The ultimate energy source is the Sun, from which plants draw energy during photosynthesis. This will be discussed in Year 6/P7 of this course, but can be discussed here if the children's enquiries, experience or knowledge require it.

Assessment of learning outcomes

a Participation in the early part of the lesson.

b Workbook page.

c Extend sheet.

UNIT 4
Living things in their environment
LESSON 11

Environmental conservation

Learning intentions

a Know why animals and plants are in danger.

b Know about the work of an environmental group.

c Think about the protection of the local environment.

Vocabulary

Conservation, danger, under threat

Lesson pattern

Whole class, Help sheet, demonstration and Workbook page, research and Extend sheet

---

RESOURCES AND SETTING UP

- Books about animals in danger and conservation.

a Help sheet.

b Workbook page. A visiting expert from an environmental group. This could be, for example, someone from the local authority dealing with litter, rubbish, or other local hazards, someone from refuse collection, or an official from an environmental agency like the Rivers Authority.

c Extend sheet.

ACTIVITIES

INTRODUCTION

- Remind the children of work they did in Year 4/P5, Unit 2 about animal conservation. If appropriate ask the children to complete the Help sheet. In subsequent discussion ensure that the children know that loss of habitat is the biggest threat to some animals. This can occur through, for example, deforestation, urban development, river pollution, sea pollution, acid rain, air pollution and modern farming. Also, tourism now disturbs some natural habitats and hunting depletes some animal populations.

- Explain that there are efforts, both large and small scale, to protect plants and animals from some of these human activities, and indeed to enhance or protect the environment for future human life.

a The children should join in the discussion on conservation and then complete the Help sheet.

b Allow the children to listen to the visiting speaker and ask questions. This talk can be the basis of an assembly or class presentation. The children should complete the Workbook page.

c The children should do some careful thinking and research about the local environment and write down some of their own ideas on the Extend sheet.

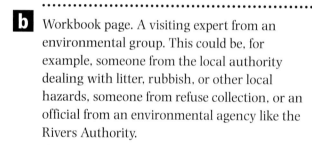

EXPECTED RESULTS

a The introduction should convey to children why living things are in danger and they should demonstrate their understanding on the Help sheet.

b The information from the visiting speaker should enlarge children's knowledge about what is being done to protect the environment.

c The children should be able to identify some local wildlife, depending on the location of the school. Measures taken could include a 'river watch', 'beach watch', litter drive, creation of wild areas in schools, parks and gardens and so on.

Assessment of learning outcomes

a Participation in discussion and/or the Help sheet.

b Workbook page.

c Extend sheet.

Review

RESOURCES AND SETTING UP

● Adjust seating arrangements to test conditions.

a **b** Workbook pages 1 and 2.

c Extend sheet.

ACTIVITIES

Ask the children to complete the Workbook pages. Those who finish can respond to the challenge on the Extend sheet.

WATCHPOINTS

● Remind the children that they can also complete their own checklist about the unit when they have time. The checklist can be found at the end of the material for this unit in the photocopiable resources.

OUTCOMES

EXPECTED ANSWERS

● Answers to the Extend sheet are as follows:

– goby – salt water fish; gaper – bi-valve mollusc; false scorpion – arachnid; frog-hopper – a bug (larva found in 'cuckoo spit'); fat hen – upright, annual plant with greenish flowers; merlin – small falcon; dunnock – hedge sparrow; muntjac – deer.

UNIT 4 Lesson 12 **Workbook 1** Stanley Thornes PRIMARY SCIENCE

1 These are the main groupings in animal classification. Fill in the names of missing kinds of group.

animal kingdom → class → order → species → genus

family

2 Why do scientists use animal and plant 'keys'? _So that they can decide on what the animal or plant is called (identify it) quickly_

3 What plant families do these belong to?

watercress _cabbage_

bramble _rose_

cowslip _primrose_

4 How do we know these are leaves from different kinds of tree?

One has small teeth round edge of leaf, different sizes?

The leaves are from trees in the same _family_ what evidence might suggest this?
The general shape and appearance of the leaves is similar

139

UNIT 4 Lesson 12 **Workbook 2** Stanley Thornes PRIMARY SCIENCE

5 How is the sea anemone adapted to life in a rock pool?
It can adhere to rocks, its tentacles pull in food, its food comes to it in the tidal water, it is camouflaged.

6 How are common bullrushes adapted to life in wet ground?
The roots tolerate being in water, leaves long, and stand upright out of water, leaves are leathery (do not let water in).

7 What does biodegradable mean? _It will 'rot' when put in the ground_

8 What can acid rain do to trees? _It can damage or kill them_

9 Write in which is predator and which is prey.

rabbit   fox

prey   _predator_

10 What is a food chain? _A string of plants and animals eaten by one another. A plant is always at the beginning._

Where do humans fit in food chains? _at the top (end)_

11 Name one of the things humans do which is a danger to animal species.
Pollute air / land / water / cut down forest / build towns / visit and trample on habitats

140

ABOUT THIS UNIT

This unit allows the children to revisit and develop further some ideas they have met in Years 3/P4 and 4/P5 of this course. They can experimentally look at the idea of sound-proofing, and begin investigating sound and pitch. They can explore shadow making and light and shade in art work. There is an opportunity to make and predict reflections in plane mirrors. The final lessons dealing with a study of light allow children access to what happens when coloured lights are mixed and allows them to make toys that use optical effects.

There follow several lessons about our universe and the solar system. The programme of study for Key Stage 2 does not set down specific requirements for knowledge of the solar system other than periodic changes of the Earth, Sun and Moon. The additional information has been included here because we feel it is of interest to children, and because it should form part of their general knowledge.

SPECIAL RESOURCES AND ADVANCED PLANNING

Lesson 1
A play telephone (made with string and a pair of paper cups or cans) is required. An alarm clock or a clock with a loud tick is also important.

Lesson 2
A tuning fork, recorder and collections of glass jars and bottles need to be assembled for this lesson.

Lesson 3
This lesson has to be carried out on a sunny day, and extra adult help would be invaluable.

Lesson 4
The classroom needs to be an art studio for the lesson. A 'still life' should be set up for the children to draw. A lamp, camera and film, a range of drawing pencils and cartridge paper are also required.

Lesson 5
Plane safety mirrors should be made available to the whole class.

Lesson 6
For this lesson powder paint and painting equipment should be set out. Also required are a room with blackout facilities, a screen, light box, colour filters and torches.

Lesson 8
A globe of the world is useful. A room with blackout facility, an overhead projector, and slide mounts are essential also.

Lesson 9
All resources available about the solar system will be useful, including information from museums and astronomy and space 'kits' that can now be bought with children in mind.

BOOK AND MULTIMEDIA SEARCH

Sound ranges
Shadows
Still life art and artists, and information/pictures about impressionists and other artists who convey light in their paintings

Mirrors/reflections
How a television works
Milky Way
Solar system
Space exploration

UNIT MAP

Lesson 1
A Know that sound travels through a medium.
b Investigate what happens when sound travels through materials.
c Find out about sound ranges.

Lesson 2
A Identify what is vibrating in the production of sounds.
b Investigate sounds using a bottle band.
c Further investigate sounds and air columns.

Lesson 3
A Look for shadows.
b Experimentally show how shadow size and shape can change.
c Explain how shadows are produced.

Lesson 4
A Look around for light and shade.
b Attempt to depict light and shade in drawings.
c Find out how artists use light and shade in their work.

Lesson 5
A Make and draw reflections.
b Predict what reflections will look like.
c Investigate reflections.

Lesson 6
A Confirm what happens when paint pigments are mixed.
b Record what happens when coloured lights are mixed.
c Find out about television screen images.

Lesson 7
A b Make toys which use optical effects.
c Know what a zoetrope is.

Lesson 8
A Know where we are in the universe.
b Know what stars and constellations are.
c Know some facts about the night sky.

Lesson 9
A Know about the solar system.
b Know some comparative facts about the planets in the solar system.
c Create a chart comparing planets.

Lesson 10
A Know what the Moon is and what it looks like.
b Describe the changes in the appearance of the Moon.
c Know about tides.

Lesson 11
A Find out about space travel and scientific discovery.
b Know of some of the discoveries made about space.
c Find out about famous astronomers.

Sound-proof?

Learning intentions

a Know that sound travels through a medium.

b Investigate what happens when sound travels through materials.

c Find out about sound ranges.

Vocabulary

Medium, sound-proof, volume (of sound)

Lesson pattern

Whole class,
Help sheet,
group work,
Workbook page,
Extend sheet

RESOURCES AND SETTING UP

a Help sheet. Work groups need: a play telephone made from two empty cans or drinking cups, joined together by a length of string attached through the base of each cup, an alarm or other clock with a loud tick.

b Workbook page. These resources are essential, for each group of five or six children in the class: a stout cardboard box with lid, cotton wool or wadding, polystyrene, clock or watch with a loud tick.

c Extend sheet. Encyclopaedias and other books containing information about sound ranges.

ACTIVITIES

INTRODUCTION

● Remind the children of the work they did on sound in Years 3/P4 and 4/P5 of this course. Ask them what is always present when a sound is made, and what is necessary for sound to travel. Check that all the children understand that sounds are caused by something vibrating (or shaking about) and that sound travels through air, water, wood and other materials. We call this the 'medium'.

● Find out whether the children know what sound-proofing is, and where we may use it. Place the ticking clock in a range of different locations around the room. The children should detect that the ticking varies in loudness (or volume), according to the surface on which the clock is placed and the material or medium around it and how far away the listener is from the sound source.

a After participating in the class discussion the children should complete the Help sheet about sound travel.

b Invite the children, in their work groups, to carry through the experiment about sound travel set out on the Workbook page.

c Using the information on the Extend sheet and from other sources, the children should be able to write about sound ranges.

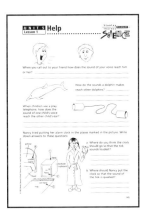

OUTCOMES

EXPECTED RESULTS

a The children should demonstrate an understanding of sound travel through a medium and the ideas involved in 'muffling' sound, by answering as follows:

- our voices travel through the air.
- dolphin sounds travel through water.
- the clock may be heard at its loudest when on or in the bedside cupboard, but sounds quieter when placed on the rug or under the pillow.

b The children may find that the polystyrene or cotton wool muffles the ticking sound more. The implications for sound-proofing a room are that walls, floors and ceilings need to have a layer of a material known to muffle sound applied to them.

c Example answers include: singing, speech, shouting, ticking watch; and infrasonic and ultrasonic are sounds outside the range heard by the human ear. Infrasonic sounds have a low frequency and ultrasonic sounds have a high frequency.

WATCHPOINTS

● Note that where there is no medium (in a vacuum) sound cannot travel. Sound travels much faster through some media than others. For example, it travels about 15 times quicker through steel than through air. Use is made of differing rates of sound travel in, for example, seismic surveying for minerals and oil, and ultrasound scanning in pregnancy.

Assessment of learning outcomes

a Involvement in discussion and Help sheet.

b Workbook page.

c Extend sheet.

Making sounds

Learning intentions

a Identify what is vibrating in the production of sounds.

b Investigate sounds using a bottle band.

c Further investigate sounds and air columns.

Vocabulary

Column of air, tuning fork, vibration

Lesson pattern

Whole class, Help sheet, group work and Workbook page, practical work and Extend sheet

---

RESOURCES AND SETTING UP

● A tuning fork and a recorder.

a Help sheet.

b Workbook page. For each work group:

four similar glass bottles or jars, jug of water, measuring jug or cylinder, ruler, metal spoon.

c Extend sheet. Bottle band containing water as used in **b**, drinking straw (preferably with a generous diameter).

ACTIVITIES

INTRODUCTION

● Remind the children of the discussion at the beginning of Lesson 1, and the points made about the presence of vibration when a sound is made. Demonstrate this by tapping the tuning fork and allowing the children to see that the 'prongs' are on the move when the sound comes out.

● Play a few notes on the recorder and establish that the children realise that the length of column of air in the instrument is vibrating (along with the instrument itself) and it is the length of the air column that determines whether a note is 'high' or 'low' (that is its pitch).

● Hand out the Help sheet and talk about the sounds being made in the picture.

a Ask the children to complete the Help sheet, so that they can confirm the presence of vibrations when sounds are made.

b In their work groups the children should collect the apparatus listed on the Workbook page and conduct the experiment to find out what happens when bottles containing differing amounts of water are tapped.

c Using the bottles from the bottle band made up in activity **b**, and a drinking straw, the children should conduct the experiment as set out on the Extend sheet.

OUTCOMES

EXPECTED RESULTS

a The information the children record on the Help sheet should include these points: **children shouting/dog barking** – vibrations in the voice box or vocal chords; **piano** – vibration of strings when tapped by the hammer operated by the piano key; **train** – there are many sources of vibration here including train body, mechanical parts and railtrack; **roadroller** – there are many sources of vibration here e.g., the mechanical parts of the machine; **drum** – vibration of the membrane; **skateboard** – vibration in board, wheels and axles; **lawnmower** – vibrations in mechanical parts.

b When tapped the bottles with less water in them should give a lower sound than those with more water in them. The children should be able to place the bottles in a row so that the sound produced gets higher along the line. They should also understand that the vibration is taking place in the column of air in the bottle.

c When the children blow across each bottle they should detect similar sound changes as those recorded above. When a straw is pushed up and down in the water, the length of the air column in the straw is changed, and the sound achieved by blowing across it will change accordingly.

WATCHPOINTS

⚠ In activities **b** and **c** tell the children not to drink the water used in the experiment.

● Food colouring can be added to the water so that the children can see the water level clearly in the bottles.

● Children must not share straws. Check that the children understand that this is what is meant by blowing across the bottles and the straw:

bottle

bottle with straw in it

● It may take some practice to get a sound to come, as those children who play an instrument requiring the use of an *embouchure* will already know.

Assessment of learning outcomes

a Help sheet.

b Workbook page.

c Extend sheet.

Shadows

Learning intentions

a Look for shadows.

b Experimentally show how shadow size and shape can change.

c Explain how shadows are produced.

Vocabulary

Cast, source

Lesson pattern

Whole class or group work,
work in pairs,
Workbook page,
Extend sheet

RESOURCES AND SETTING UP

a Help sheet. Poster 5.3. A sunny day, producing shadows, is required for this lesson. It may be a good idea to have extra adult help for the first part of the lesson so that the children can walk around school in groups. (See activity **A** for what to do in the absence of sunshine.)

b Workbook page.

A room with blackout (dim light is required), pocket torches (at least one between two for the whole class), card or sugar paper.

c Extend sheet.

ACTIVITIES

INTRODUCTION

● Show the children Poster 5.3. Ask the children to identify what is happening in the pictures. Here are some example questions:

What do you need to make a shadow?
What is a shadow?
Why do shadows vary in length?

● If you have extra adult help place the children in work groups, otherwise take the children as a whole class group into activity **A**.

 Let the children walk around the school, looking for shadows cast by the sunlight, both inside and outside the building. It may be appropriate to give the children the Help sheet at the outset, or they can complete it when they return to the classroom. If the weather is not sunny, and the lesson cannot be moved to a sunny day, give the children torches to experiment with in a dim room, before tackling the Help sheet.

b Ask the children to work in pairs. Reduce light levels in the room and allow the children to work on the task set out on the Workbook page, where they are required to make a shadow of a cut-out shape and investigate factors affecting the shadow.

c The children are required to draw a picture and write an explanation for how a shadow occurs on the Extend sheet.

OUTCOMES

EXPECTED RESULTS

 The notes the children make will depend on their interests and what they have seen. Suggested points to raise in answer to the margin questions are as follows:

– 'sunshine' comes from the Sun.
– the shadow is made on the side away from the Sun.
– the length of shadow depends on the direction of the Sun's rays.
– a shadow happens where the sunlight cannot reach.
– shadows only occur in the light, at night there are no shadows.
– shadows are less distinct when sunlight is diffuse.

b The children should note the following on the Workbook page:

– the shadow is the same shape as the cut-out.
– the shadow gets smaller when moved further from the light source.
– the shadow gets larger when moved nearer the light source.

c You need a light source and an object placed in the path of the light rays to make a shadow. The light cannot go through or around the object, so there is an area of darkness beyond the object which is its shadow.

WATCHPOINTS

 Warn the children against looking directly at the Sun with the naked eye. It can damage eyesight.

Assessment of learning outcomes

a Involvement and contribution during the walk around school and the Help sheet.

b Practical work and Workbook page.

c Extend sheet.

Light and shading

Learning intentions

a Look around for light and shade.

b Attempt to depict light and shade in drawings.

c Find out how artists use light and shade in their work.

Vocabulary

Media, shading, still life, 'weight' of paper

Lesson pattern

Whole class, practical work, Workbook page, Extend sheet

RESOURCES AND SETTING UP

a A room with curtains or blinds is important for this lesson, so that areas of shadow can be created. Set up a 'still life' for the children to draw. This can match those we find amongst great paintings, or include children's belongings or things from around the classroom, in addition to the more common inanimate objects like fruit and flowers. Lamp, range of drawing pencils for the children to try, cartridge paper, camera and film.

b Workbook page.

c Extend sheet. Books about art and artists, including reproductions of pencil drawings.

ACTIVITIES

INTRODUCTION

● Show the children the still life set up in the classroom and move into activity **A**.

a Dim the light levels in the room sufficiently to make clear areas of shadow with a lamp. Shine the lamp on the still life and point out the areas of light and shade. Let the children look very carefully, so that they can see the 'highlights' on shiny things like fruits or metal, and the areas of dark and lighter shade. Move the lamp around so that the areas of shadow are changed. Set the lamp so that a good composition is achieved. Ask the children to do task **b**.

b Let the children draw the still life, using a variety of pencils. Ask them to be particularly careful to show the areas of light and shade in their picture. Afterwards they can complete the Workbook page.

c Ask the children to find out about the use of pencil and light and shade in great artworks, using resource books and recording their findings on the Extend sheet.

OUTCOMES

EXPECTED RESULTS

a With help the children should become adept at identifying light and shade.

b The children should be able to attempt pencil shading to depict shade and leave lighter areas to show light in their pictures.

c The artists and work selected will depend on the resources the children access.

WATCHPOINTS

● Pencils are available in grades in the ranges 6B to B, HB, F and H to 9H. B (b stands for 'black') pencils are 'softer', easier to make a mark with and do not keep a point long. H pencils are 'harder'.

● Paper weights are judged by the weight of the ream. A heavier paper is therefore likely to be thicker.

● If there is a camera and film available, try taking some photographs of the still life, when lit in a range of ways. These photographs can be displayed alongside the children's own drawings.

Assessment of learning outcomes

a Participation in activity **A**.

b Drawing and Workbook page.

c Extend sheet.

Reflections

Learning intentions

a Make and draw reflections.

b Predict what reflections will look like.

c Investigate reflections.

Vocabulary

Plane, reflection

Lesson pattern

Practical work and Help sheet,
Workbook page and practical work,
Practical work and Extend sheet

RESOURCES AND SETTING UP

a Help sheet.

Plane safety mirrors (enough for each child in the class to have one), resource boxes of small items (one box per work group). The box could contain things like these: paper clips, corks, bottle tops, buttons, badges, pencils, play coins, hair slides, card shapes.

b Workbook page. Mirrors as in .

c Extend sheet. Two plane safety mirrors for each child.

ACTIVITIES

INTRODUCTION

● The first activity of the lesson is exploratory, and should build on work the children have done in Year 3/P4 of this course. The children can therefore go straight into it.

a The children should explore and record work on reflections on the Help sheet.

b For this task the children are required to make predictions about reflections. It would be better if mirrors were put aside for the first part of the task. Work should be recorded on the Workbook page.

c Following the instructions on the Extend sheet the children should conduct the two-mirror investigations set out there.

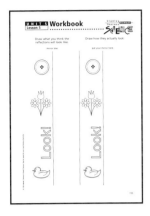

OUTCOMES

EXPECTED RESULTS

a The children should indicate that the reflection is seen as far behind the mirror line as the object is in front, and there is a match of object and reflection.

b This is quite a demanding task and the children may find they need to explore reflections more before they get their predictions of reflections correct.

c The answers should contain these ideas:

a reflection of a face is 'the other way round'. Light from the object reaches the mirror and is reflected off the mirror into the eye. The mirrors need to be held facing one another and in parallel as shown here.

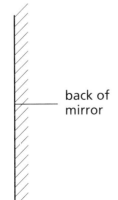

back of mirror

WATCHPOINTS

⚠ Bind the edges of glass mirrors with masking or insulating tape.

● These concepts may help the assessment of results on the Extend sheet.

- the apparent reversal in the mirror is called lateral inversion.
- the angle at which light reaches the mirror (angle of incidence) is equal to the angle of reflection.
- the mirrors need to be held as in a periscope.

Assessment of learning outcomes

a Help sheet.

b Workbook page (though not all reflections may be accurate).

c Extend sheet.

Colour mix

Learning intentions

a Confirm what happens when paint pigments are mixed.

b Record what happens when coloured lights are mixed.

c Find out about television screen images.

Vocabulary

Cyan, filter, light box, magenta, pigment, primary, secondary

Lesson pattern

Demonstration or practical work, Help sheet, demonstration, Workbook page, research and Extend sheet

RESOURCES AND SETTING UP

a Help sheet. Mixed powder paint in primary colours. Palettes or old plates, brushes and water for brush cleaning.

b Workbook page. Room with blackout facilities, screen, light box with colour filters, torches.

c Extend sheet. Books containing information about television pictures.

ACTIVITIES

INTRODUCTION

● Explain to the children that the key idea in the lesson is to examine and compare what happens when colours of paint pigment and colours of light are mixed.

a The children should either watch a demonstration by the teacher or conduct the following experiment themselves. Mix together the colours red, blue and yellow paint in pairs and observe the colours made. Then mix all three colours and see what happens. Complete the Help sheet with the outcomes.

b The children may recall looking at colours of light in Year 3/P4 of this course. Black the room out and erect the screen and light box. Place filters in turn in the light box and hold filters over torches. Let the children see what happens when light is mixed in the following ways:

red and blue
blue and green
red and green
red, blue and green.

Give the children copies of the Workbook page so that they can record the outcomes.

c Invite the children to look up how television pictures are made and record what they find out on the Extend sheet.

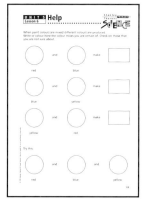

OUTCOMES

EXPECTED RESULTS

a Red and blue make purple; blue and yellow make green; yellow and red make orange. Red, blue and yellow will make some sort of sludgy brown-black, depending on the colour shades mixed.

b (1) red and blue make magenta; (2) blue and green make cyan; (3) red and green make yellow; (4) red, blue and green make white light; (5) red, blue and green are primary colours of light; (6) paint box primary colours are red, blue and yellow; (7) the secondary colours of light are magenta, cyan and yellow.

c The key points the children may find are that colour television pictures are made of tiny strips of primary colour light. At a distance strips close to one another combine to give secondary colours.

Assessment of learning outcomes

a Help sheet.

b Workbook page.

c Extend sheet.

Optical toys

Learning intentions

a **b** Make toys which use optical effects.

c Know what a zoetrope is.

Vocabulary

Flicker, optical illusion, optics, persistence of vision, thaumatrope, zoetrope

Lesson pattern

Whole class, Help sheet, Workbook page, Extend sheet

RESOURCES AND SETTING UP

a Help sheet. Card, rubber bands, scissors.

b Workbook page. Paper fasteners.

c Extend sheet

ACTIVITIES

INTRODUCTION

● Remind the children of the work they have done on optical illusions in Year 4/ P5 of this course. Ask them what optical illusions are. Tell the children that this lesson focuses on the kind of illusion that is related to the working of our eyes. The children will probably know that cinema film is a series of still pictures which appear on the screen in turn. We see these pictures as depicting movement because of our sight. When we look at something a little 'picture' of the object appears at the back of the eye. This is held there for part of a second; long enough for it to combine with the 'picture' of something else if it is put before our eyes quickly. Tell the children the two toys they will make use the 'cinema film' idea.

a The children are asked to follow the directions on the Help sheet in order to make a 'twizzle toy'. If it is appropriate the images on the Help sheet can be masked so that the children can draw in their own pictures.

b The children should draw the pictures to make up the pages of a flicker book on the Workbook page. Remind them that the pictures should be near the bottom edge of the page, and the best action is achieved by making the picture change very little from one drawing to the next. These can be cut out and fixed together.

c The Extend sheet depicts a zoetrope and its design. The children should look carefully at the picture and write how it works and how it compares with the toys produced in **a** and **b** above.

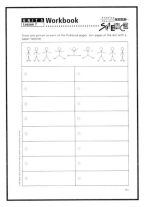
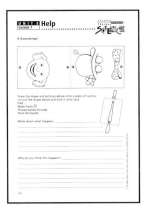

OUTCOMES

EXPECTED RESULTS

a When the rubber bands are twisted between the fingers, the pictures on both sides of the card look as though they appear together and make one picture.

b The book is 'flicked' to show the pictures which should give the illusion of movement.

c The zoetrope works by rotating the cylinder drum while viewing the picture by looking through a slot on the other side of the cylinder. One picture is 'held' by the eye and the next picture comes into view. If the cylinder is turned at the right speed the pictures will give the illusion of movement. This is why the zoetrope is similar to the thaumatrope and the flicker book. It uses the phenomenon of persistence of vision.

WATCHPOINTS

● A thaumaturge means 'wonder worker'; so this toy is seen as 'miraculous'. The -'trope' in both thaumatrope and zoetrope is from the Greek 'turn'.

Assessment of learning outcomes

a **b** Involvement in introductory discussion, the working thaumatrope and the working flicker book.

c Extend sheet.

Us and the stars

Learning intentions

a Know where we are in the universe.

b Know what stars and constellations are.

c Know some facts about the night sky.

Vocabulary

Constellation, Earth, galaxy, location, Moon, planet, solar system, space, star, Sun

Lesson pattern

Whole class,
Help sheet,
whole class discussion,
demonstration and/or
Workbook page,
Extend sheet

RESOURCES AND SETTING UP

● Poster 5.8.

a Help sheet. A globe.

b Workbook page. A room with blackout facilities, an overhead projector, slide mounts.

c Extend sheet. Books about the solar system. Books about stars and the night sky.

ACTIVITIES

INTRODUCTION

● Talk to the children about where we are in the universe. With the children's help, write an address on the blackboard or a large sheet of paper. Begin with the school address and then go progressively outwards to reveal something like this:

Mrs Twig's Class
Hazelwood County Primary School
Treesville
Leafshire ZZ1 2YX
England
U.K.
Planet Earth

Our Full Address

Invite the children to complete the Help sheet.

a After the initial discussion, the children should complete the Help sheet, setting out their location in the universe.

b Check that the blackout and slide projector work. Gather the children together. Find out what they know about the night sky. Show the children Poster 5.8. Tell the children that the Earth is a planet. What we see in the night sky is our Moon and stars. Stars are made of gases. The Sun is a star. A group of stars is a constellation. Some of these have been given animal names. Let the children look at some patterns of stars by placing the constellation cards you have made in the slide projector. Let the children try to identify some of those on the Workbook page.

c The children should use books to search for the information on the Extend sheet so that they can join up and complete the space facts.

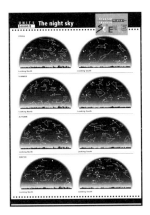 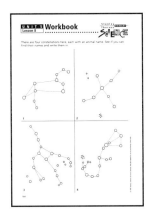  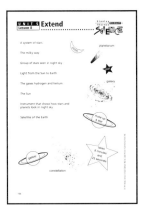

OUTCOMES

EXPECTED RESULTS

a The children should confirm that they understand their location by completing their 'address' on the Help sheet.

b The cards with pin holes in them placed in the projector should reveal light patterns on the screen that look a little like star constellations. The constellations on the Workbook page are **1** the lion (Leo), **2** the swan (Cygnus), **3** the great bear (Ursa Major) and **4** the scorpion (Scorpio).

c The space facts should read as follows:

- a system of stars – galaxy
- the Milky Way – galaxy
- group of stars seen in the night sky – constellation
- light from the Sun to Earth takes 8 minutes and 23 seconds
- the gases hydrogen and helium make up a star
- the Sun is a star
- instrument that shows how stars and planets look in the night sky – planetarium
- satellite of the Earth – Moon.

WATCHPOINTS

● If the slide projector is not available, allow the children to look carefully at some star constellations in books and try naming those on the Workbook page.

● In preparation, cut pieces of card to fit slide mounts. Pencil in star constellations on the cards. Push pin holes through the card to mark the star positions.

Assessment of learning outcomes

a Help sheet.

b Involvement in discussion, demonstration and the Workbook page.

c Extend sheet.

Planets

Learning intentions

a Know about the solar system.

b Know some comparative facts about the planets in the solar system.

c Create a chart comparing planets.

Vocabulary

Names of planets in the solar system

Lesson pattern

Whole class,
Help sheet,
group work,
Workbook page
presentation,
Extend sheet

RESOURCES AND SETTING UP

● Pictures of the planets in the solar system. Books with detailed information on the planets in the solar system.
Arrange a display of books and pictures for the children to use during the lesson.

● Alternatively set the room up for a 'workshop' where children can visit different parts of the room to obtain items of information. There could, for example, be data about sizes and distances in one corner, appearance and composition in another, orbit and revolution in another. Or all the information on Mars and Venus could be assembled in one location and other planets in other locations.

a Help sheet.

b Workbook page. Rough paper. The children may require music or other resources for their presentation.

c Extend sheet.

ACTIVITIES

INTRODUCTION

● Show the children pictures and charts depicting the planets in the solar system. Talk through the names of these. Look at the position of the Earth in relation to other planets. Examine which is furthest from the Sun, which is likely to be the hottest, which have rings around them and so on. Invite the children to see if they can now name the planets on the Help sheet.

a The children should fill in the names of the planets on the Help sheet.

b In their work groups the children should make a study of a planet. Make up to eight groups and ask each group to choose a different planet. Tell each group they have a short while to find out some important facts about their planet and plan a presentation to the class. The Workbook page may help the children focus on some important facts. (The Earth has been omitted from this Workbook page so that the children can get to know about the other planets in the solar system.)

c Invite the children to use information they have now gleaned about several planets to create a comparative chart on the Extend sheet.

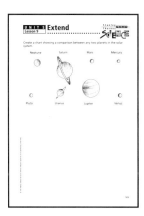

OUTCOMES

EXPECTED RESULTS

a The names of the planets are as follows starting with the one nearest to the Sun: Mercury, Venus, Earth, Mars, Jupiter, Saturn, Uranus, Neptune, Pluto.

b The presentation will vary according to the resources used and what the children regard as important facts. They may, for example, do a movement sequence to show the orbit of the planet, or they may draw rough pictures, play music or give a talk.

c These will depend on the kinds of information the children have accessed, and should be checked against their sources.

WATCHPOINTS

● Mixed ability groups may work well for the presentation in **b**, or the teacher can help out in presenting the work of groups who find this difficult.

● There is much to do in this lesson. Those children who wish to pursue their study further could take the Extend sheet home to complete a comparative chart from what they have learned and their own researches.

Assessment of learning outcomes

a Help sheet.

b Workbook page.

c Extend sheet.

The Earth's Moon

Learning intentions

a Know what the Moon is and what it looks like.

b Describe the changes in the appearance of the Moon.

c Know about tides.

Vocabulary

Crescent, full, gibbous, Moon, phase

Lesson pattern

Whole class,
Help sheet,
whole class,
Workbook page,
Extend sheet

RESOURCES AND SETTING UP

● Poster 5.10.
Books about the Moon.

a Help sheet.

b Workbook page.

c Extend sheet.

ACTIVITIES

INTRODUCTION

● Show the children Poster 5.10 and talk about the Moon. Find out what the children know about the Moon and its orbit and rotation. Tell the children some more facts about the Moon. Here are some examples:

– the Moon is a satellite of the Earth.
– it is dry with no atmosphere.
– it goes round the Earth every 27.3 days.
– it rotates on its axis every 27.3 days also and so only one side of the Moon is seen from Earth.

a Hand out copies of the Help sheet to the children and either discuss this in a whole class group, comparing it with Poster 5.10 or let the children talk about what they see in their work groups.

b Talk to the children about the changes we see in the appearance of the Moon in the sky. The children should write about what they have noticed about how the Moon looks in the sky on the Workbook page.

c The children are required to draw on their understanding of life and environment to speculate on the effects of tides. They can record their thoughts on the Extend sheet.

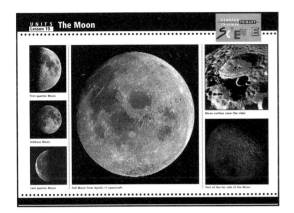

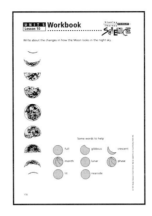

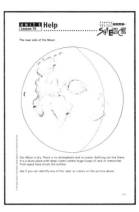

OUTCOMES

EXPECTED RESULTS

a Check that the children understand that the picture on the Help sheet (labelled version opposite) is the only part of the Moon we see, and that we can only see the Moon by light reflected from the Sun.

b The discussion can be descriptive rather than explanatory. These are the important points:

– the shape of the Moon appears to change from night to night.
– the Moon stays the same shape but what we see of it changes.
– the appearance of the Moon changes over a month.
– the changes in appearance are called phases. Crescent (less than half Moon), gibbous (half or more) and full (whole) are words used for what we see of the Moon.

c At low tide the sea recedes exposing land (the beach). At high tide the sea moves up the beach covering more of the land. The effects of tidal movement are felt by plants and animals living on the shore line, including rock pool dwellers and sea birds. Plant life and growth is affected. Over time the movements of the sea cause erosion and deposition and affect the shape of the landscape. Thus the Moon has an effect on land shape and plant and animal habitats.

WATCHPOINTS

● There are complex ideas in this lesson, and it is intended that the children should be introduced to them here. Explanations should come in Year 6/P7 of this course.

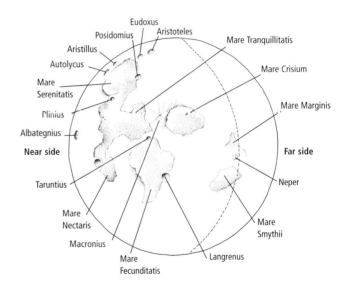

Assessment of learning outcomes

a Participation in discussion and attention to the Help sheet.

b Workbook page.

c Extend sheet.

Space discoveries

Learning intentions

a Find out about space travel and scientific discovery.

b Know of some of the discoveries made about space.

c Find out about famous astronomers.

Vocabulary

Astronaut, shuttle, telescope, other vocabulary about space that the children find and use

Lesson pattern

Whole class and Help sheet, Workbook page, Extend sheet

RESOURCES AND SETTING UP

● Mount a classroom display of all the school resources about space. Include books and posters and ask the children to bring in space toys they have. If there is any topical news about space travel include press cuttings. Research and resource the following space phenomena: black hole, meteorite, comet, asteroid.

● If a display is not possible books about space travel and discovery are still essential.

a Help sheet.

b Workbook page.

c Extend sheet. Books about famous people in history, and about the history of astronomy.

ACTIVITIES

INTRODUCTION

● Discuss the resources set out on display. Find out what the children know about space travel. Hand around the Help sheet and talk over the images there.

a The children are required to inspect the classroom display and talk about the images on the Help sheet.

b The children should research the space phenomena listed on the Workbook page.

c Using biographical resources the children should find out about two of the famous people who made contributions to astronomy and whose pictures appear on the Extend sheet.

OUTCOMES

EXPECTED RESULTS

 The points that emerge in discussion will depend on the children's interests and the resources set on display.

b Here are some of the facts the children may list on the Workbook page.

Black holes: form when stars explode; have such strong gravity that even light cannot escape – black holes are therefore invisible.

Meteorite: meteors are dust or small stones (maybe bits of asteroids); when they enter the Earth's atmosphere they get hot and show as a 'shooting star'. Those that reach Earth are called meteorites.

Comet: made of frozen gases and dust; thought to come from the cloud around the solar system; when a comet gets near the Sun it gets very hot, its surface turns to gas making it shine and have a dust and gas 'tail'.

Asteroid: pieces of rock, up to aproximately 1,000 km across. Many orbit the Sun in the asteroid belt.

c Some famous people in astronomy include:

– Copernicus (1473–1543). Polish astronomer, suggested the planets in the solar system orbited the Sun.

– Brahe (1546–1601). Danish astronomer, observed a new star (named after him) devised star charts.
– Kepler (1571–1630). German astronomer whose work laid the groundwork for Newton's discoveries. Kepler's work was the starting point for modern astronomy.
– Galileo (1564–1642). Italian astronomer, mathematician and natural philosopher, made many discoveries; for example, said the Moon's 'shine' is reflected light and the marks on it are mountains and valleys, also discovered the satellites of Jupiter and sunspots.
– Newton (1642–1727). English scientist and mathematician, invented a telescope that uses mirrors.

Assessment of learning outcomes

a Involvement in early part of the lesson and attention to the resources on display.

b Workbook page.

c Extend sheet.

Review

RESOURCES AND SETTING UP

- Adjust seating arrangements to test conditions.

....
a **b** Workbook pages 1 and 2.

....
c Extend sheet.

ACTIVITIES

Ask the children to complete the Workbook pages. Those who finish can respond to the challenge on the Extend sheet.

WATCHPOINTS

- Remind the children that they can also complete their own checklist about the unit when they have time. The checklist can be found at the end of the material for this unit in the photocopiable resources.

OUTCOMES

EXPECTED ANSWERS

● Information entered on the Extend sheet will depend on the children's own interests and sources used.

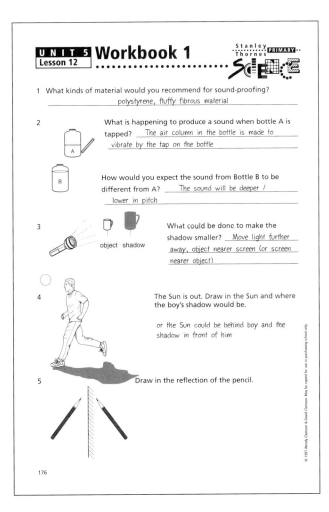

UNIT 5 Lesson 12 — **Workbook 1**
Stanley Thornes PRIMARY Science

1 What kinds of material would you recommend for sound-proofing?
polystyrene, fluffy fibrous material

2 What is happening to produce a sound when bottle A is tapped? _The air column in the bottle is made to vibrate by the tap on the bottle_

How would you expect the sound from Bottle B to be different from A? _The sound will be deeper / lower in pitch_

3 object shadow What could be done to make the shadow smaller? _Move light further away, object nearer screen (or screen nearer object)_

4 The Sun is out. Draw in the Sun and where the boy's shadow would be.

or the Sun could be behind boy and the shadow in front of him

5 Draw in the reflection of the pencil.

176

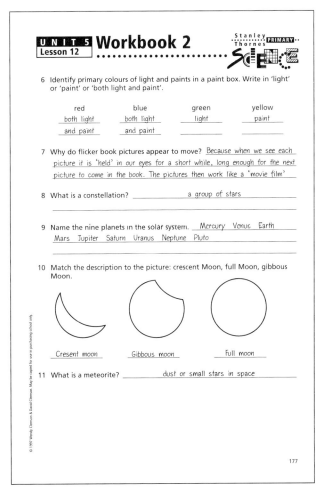

UNIT 5 Lesson 12 — **Workbook 2**
Stanley Thornes PRIMARY Science

6 Identify primary colours of light and paints in a paint box. Write in 'light' or 'paint' or 'both light and paint'.

red	blue	green	yellow
both light and paint	_both light and paint_	_light_	_paint_

7 Why do flicker book pictures appear to move? _Because when we see each picture it is 'held' in our eyes for a short while, long enough for the next picture to come in the book. The pictures then work like a 'movie film'_

8 What is a constellation? _a group of stars_

9 Name the nine planets in the solar system. _Mercury Venus Earth Mars Jupiter Saturn Uranus Neptune Pluto_

10 Match the description to the picture: crescent Moon, full Moon, gibbous Moon.

Cresent moon   _Gibbous moon_   _Full moon_

11 What is a meteorite? _dust or small stars in space_

177

© 1997 Wendy Clemson & David Clemson. May be copied for use in purchasing school only.

ABOUT THIS UNIT

The intention in this unit is to continue to develop and consolidate the scientific skills the children have acquired during previous years and throughout Year 5/P6. There are opportunities here to do a good deal of thinking about the processes involved in scientific enquiry. Experimental planning, the conduct of fair tests, data presentation and interpretation, choice of apparatus and the drawing of conclusions are all explicitly presented to the children.

SPECIAL RESOURCES AND ADVANCED PLANNING

Lesson 1
Fresh leaves from a tree or a range of trees are required here. Access to the trees may also be required, depending on the investigation the children decide to carry through.

Lesson 2
Bread making recipe and ingredients including dried yeast, along with kitchen equipment and access to an oven to cook loaves in. Extra adult help is not essential, but invaluable in cooking the bread.

Lesson 3
Samples of table salt, caster sugar and another soluble crystalline substance like bath salts or lemonade crystals are required for this lesson.

Lesson 4
Balls made from different materials (e.g. rubber, plastic); enough for each pair or work group to have three different ones are necessary for this lesson.

Lesson 5
Thermometers suitable for accurately reading temperatures on the 20-90° C range should be available to the children in this lesson.

Lesson 6
Dinner registers for all the classes in the school should be borrowed for this lesson. The relevant pages can be photocopied if this is more convenient.

Lesson 7
Magnifiers giving different strengths of magnification, three for each group attempting this experiment. The magnifiers should, ideally be all the same size.

Lesson 8
A wide variety of apparatus is necessary for this lesson including the following: measuring cylinders, beakers, washing bowls, teapots and mugs, Newton meters, string, clamps and clamp stands, thermometers, timers, aquaria, cocktail sticks, blindfold.

Lesson 9
Marbles of different sizes, small wooden blocks, and a space large enough for all the children to allow the marbles to run down the ramp and come to rest are necessary for this lesson.

Lesson 10
Before the lesson collect finger prints from a number of people. They could be children in the class or members of staff or of the family. Water-based ink can be used so that it is easier to wash off the fingers after printing. Sugar coated chocolate buttons are also required here.

BOOK AND MULTIMEDIA SEARCH

Bread making
Graph computer package
Famous scientists

UNIT MAP

Lesson 1
A Suggest ideas for experiments.
b Carry through an experiment based on own ideas.
c Evaluate classroom experiments.

Lesson 2
A Distinguish scientific predictions.
b Make predictions about experimental outcomes.
c Devise further experiments.

Lesson 3
A Define a fair test.
b Devise and conduct a fair test.
c Identify fair tests that could be done in specific settings.

Lesson 4
A Interpret tables and bar charts.
b Create tables and bar charts.
c Interpret pictorial representations.

Lesson 5
A Know how to draw a line graph.
b Create a line graph.
c Interpret a line graph.

Lesson 6
A Identify data patterns.
b Collate data sets revealing patterns.
c Identify data sets that may yield patterns.

Lesson 7
A Identify key factors in experiments.
b Carry through an experiment noting key factors.
c Devise an experiment isolating key factors.

Lesson 8
A Identify measures to be made in an experiment.
b Choose appropriate apparatus for an experiment.
c Improve on choices of experimental apparatus.

Lesson 9
A Know why experiments are repeated.
b Repeat an experiment.
c Collate results of repeated experiments.

Lesson 10
A Know what a 'conclusion' is.
b Draw conclusions.
c Know how conclusions can be modified.

Lesson 11
A Know of the importance of the work of some scientists.
b Find out about the life and work of a famous scientist.
c Complete a scientific apparatus quiz.

Scientific ideas

Learning intentions

a Suggest ideas for experiments.

b Carry through an experiment based on own ideas.

c Evaluate classroom experiments.

Vocabulary

Evaluation, experiment, outcomes, names for sample trees used in the lesson

Lesson pattern

Whole class and the Help sheet, practical groupwork and Workbook page, Extend sheet

RESOURCES AND SETTING UP

a Help sheet. Fresh leaves from a tree or a range of trees are required here.

b Workbook page. Leaves as in **A** above. Access to the trees may also be required, depending on the investigation the children decide to carry through. Squared paper, 30 cm rulers and other measuring instruments. Additional apparatus may be required depending on what the children decide to do.

c Extend sheet.

ACTIVITIES

INTRODUCTION

● Supply each child with a copy of the Help sheet and in a whole class discuss the kinds of investigations the children would like to conduct. Examine some of the sample leaves in front of the children to stimulate the production of experimental ideas.

a The children should take part in the initial discussion and put forward ideas.

b In their work groups the children should try to carry through one of the ideas suggested in the introduction, writing what they did on the Workbook page.

c The children should reflect on the investigation they have done and evaluate it, recording their comments on the Extend sheet.

OUTCOMES

EXPECTED RESULTS

 The children's ideas for investigations can be listed on the board, and may include things like this.

- How many leaves are there on a tree?
- Are all the leaves on a tree the same size and shape?
- What leaf shapes are there on school field trees?
- Is there any evidence of the health or age of the tree?
- What is living in the leaf mould under the tree? (If leaf mould is still available.)

b The results will depend on the ideas the children are investigating and the way they decide to carry them through.

c Comments will depend on the strategies tried by the children.

WATCHPOINTS

● Mixed ability grouping may be appropriate for activity **b**.

 Ensure children wash their hands with soap and water after handling the plant material.

Assessment of learning outcomes

a Participation in the introductory discussion.

b Workbook page.

c Extend sheet.

Prediction

Learning intentions

 Distinguish scientific predictions.

 Make predictions about experimental outcomes.

c Devise further experiments.

Vocabulary

Irreversible change, predict, prediction, 'prove', yeast

Lesson pattern

Whole class discussion, Help sheet, Workbook page and demonstration, Extend sheet

RESOURCES AND SETTING UP

a Help sheet.

 Workbook page. Bread making recipe and ingredients are needed, including dried yeast, jug, warm water, bowl, board on which to knead the dough access to an oven to cook loaves in. Extra adult help is not essential but invaluable in cooking the bread.

c Extend sheet.

b Call the children together to observe one step in the bread making. They can then complete the Workbook page.

c The children who complete activity **b** can go on to formulate additional experiments which can be written up on the Extend sheet.

ACTIVITIES

INTRODUCTION

● Ask the children what they understand by the word prediction. Discuss the suggestions for predictions set out on the Help sheet. Create some new ones based on the class, the weather or other topical data of relevance to the children.

 The children should, in a whole class group, join in a discussion concerning predictions. They are then asked to complete the Help sheet and make predictions of their own. Ask them to see if they can predict things that it would be possible to find out relatively easily.

OUTCOMES

EXPECTED RESULTS

 The statements on the Help sheet that are predictions are as follows: it often rains during this part of the year so I think it is possible it will rain tomorrow. I predict that one of the ingredients in custard makes it yellow.

This is a prediction that needs more detail to make it testable: books with more pages are heavier (for example, are the books paper or hard back? What about book size as opposed to length?).

These are predictions that seem unlikely (and the second needs modification to make it testable): most baby boys will be called Kevin next year. Green will always be the colour of envy and jealousy.

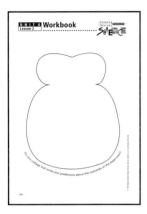

This is not a prediction but a statement of fact: my friend Jack wears size 5 boots.

The children's own predictions will vary.

b The children should predict that the yeast will make the bread dough rise, and the resulting loaf will be soft with 'holes' in the interior.

c The experiments that the children suggest may include things like:

- vary the amount of yeast.
- vary the amount of water.
- vary the temperature for 'proving'.
- vary the temperature for baking.

WATCHPOINTS

- A prediction is a statement about something that may occur in the future. It is scientific if it is based on factual evidence. It is possible to test if it has been set down exactly and can be carried through within the constraints on the experimenter (time, budget, access to information, etc.).

- Read the bread recipe instructions and work out timings for the cooking. The children should, at some points in the school day, have a chance to see the action of the yeast, the results of 'proving' the dough and the appearance of the finished loaf.

Here is a typical bread recipe:

675 g strong white flour
salt
20 g butter
dried yeast

Rub the butter into the flour and salt until the mix is like breadcrumbs. Add the yeast. Mix and knead until the dough forms into a ball. Knead on a board for about 4 minutes. Place in a bowl. Cover with a cloth and leave in a warm place for about $1-1\frac{1}{2}$ hours (until doubled in size). Halve the dough and make into lozenge shapes to fit two small loaf tins. Cover each tin with clear film which has a little oil on it. Leave tins in a warm place for about half an hour. Take off the clear film. Cook at gas mark 8, 230° C for 20–30 minutes.

⚠️ Use cooking equipment, not science equipment for this activity. Ensure cleanliness of equipment, surfaces and children's hands.

Assessment of learning outcomes

a Involvement in early discussion and the Help sheet.

b Workbook page.

c Extend sheet.

What is fair?

Learning intentions

a Define a fair test.

b Devise and conduct a fair test.

c Identify fair tests that could be done in specific settings.

Vocabulary

'Control', dissolve, fair test, replicate, saturate, solution

Lesson pattern

Whole class, practical work in work group and Workbook page, Extend sheet

RESOURCES AND SETTING UP

a Help sheet.

b Workbook page. For each work group the following apparatus is required: samples of table salt, caster sugar and other soluble crystalline substance (e.g. lemonade crystals, bath salts), with no identifying labels or packs, beakers, a jug of water, teaspoon, access to a sink, paper towels, measuring cylinder or jug.

ACTIVITIES

INTRODUCTION

● Ask the children what they understand by a 'fair test'. They may recall the work they did in Year 4/P5, Unit 6 and work in other units both in Year 4/P5 and in this current year where 'fair tests' have been discussed.

a Hand out copies of the Help sheet and ask for the children's comments. Discuss what is meant by 'control' and 'replicate'.

b Invite the children, in their work groups, to conduct the experiment on solubility and saturation set out on the Workbook page. In Unit 1 this year they will have done experiments on solubility, so they should be able to conduct the experiment in a manner which makes it a 'fair test'.

c The groups who finish the experiment in **b** can look carefully at the settings described on the Extend sheet and try working out some experiments. This could be done collaboratively.

OUTCOMES

EXPECTED RESULTS

 The children may be able to add more points to the list of items on the Help sheet, confirming the nature of a 'fair test'.

b All three substances dissolve in water. In trials more sugar dissolved in a fixed amount of water than salt or bath salts. Results may vary according to the exact materials used and the temperature of the water. Results within the class, in similar conditions should be similar.

c The 'fair tests' suggested by the children may vary. Here are some suggestions.

Similar specimens of the same species of plants could be reared indoors and outdoors. Those indoors might have the moisture content of their soil matched to conditions outside. How much light both sets of plants get should be considered. Temperature readings of indoor and outdoor temperatures throughout the day and night may also be useful.

Liz may get wetter because she is taller. Is one of these people fatter than the other? What are they wearing? Measurements could be taken of the angle of the umbrellas, the direction of the rain (and wind if there is any). Both people could have their height measured with and without the umbrella held in position. It may then be possible to say whether the rain gets beneath umbrellas held by taller people.

The composition of the bowl and wafer are unclear. Both need to be placed in similar conditions. A decision needs to be made about how to judge melting rates. This setting is closest to a fair test.

WATCHPOINTS

● A 'control' is an experimental sample which receives exactly the same treatment as the experimental sample(s) except for the action to be tested. A 'control' is not always required in 'fair tests'. In fact there is no control in the experiment done in activity **b** here. In the absence of a control, all experimental samples should be subjected to the same treatment in similar conditions.

Assessment of learning outcomes

 Involvement in the introductory discussion.

b Participation in the experiment in **b** and evidence that care was taken to make the experiment 'fair'.

c This task is very demanding. There should be some evidence that the child has started to think about the issues in planning 'fair tests'.

Tables and charts

Learning intentions

a Interpret tables and bar charts.

b Create tables and bar charts.

c Interpret pictorial representations.

Vocabulary

Bar chart, table, trial

Lesson pattern

Whole class or work groups and Help sheet, whole class, practical work in pairs or work groups and Workbook page, Extend sheet

RESOURCES AND SETTING UP

a Help sheet.

b Workbook page. Balls made from different materials (e.g. rubber, plastic); enough for each pair or work group to have three different ones. Metre sticks and measuring tapes.

c Extend sheet.

ACTIVITIES

INTRODUCTION

● Either in a whole class group, or in work groups allow the children to talk over their ideas about the results set out on the Help sheet. Draw together these ideas and interpretations.

a The children should take part in an analysis of the results available on the Help sheet. The teacher can ask quick fire questions like the following.

What was the furthest distance flown by John's aeroplane?
Which plane flew furthest of all?

What was the total distance travelled by John's plane in all three trials?
Could the children have measured the height of their planes?
Do you think it mattered where the planes were launched from?
Could the height of launch make a difference?

How many butterflies visited Steve's bush?
Which kind of insect made fewest visits?
How many 'bee visits' were there?

b Give the children, in pairs or groups, a selection of balls to experiment with. Allow the children to conduct the experiment, finding how high each ball bounces over a number of trials. The children can record their results on the Workbook page, in rough and make a table on a second sheet of paper, or the table can be constructed on the Workbook page.

c The children should inspect the pictorial representation on the Extend sheet and make some interpretations.

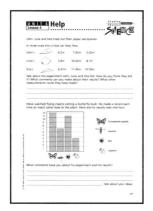

OUTCOMES

EXPECTED RESULTS

 It is expected that in a group or whole class setting, most of the children should be able to make sense of the results presented. There may also be further discussion about how they themselves would do the experiments, and how they could be made 'fair tests'. For example, the children may choose for all planes to be launched in the same way, at the same spot, by the same child. They may choose to fly the planes indoors to limit air movement changes.

They may consider that Steve should see whether these sightings are of different or the same insect each time. They may consider this impossible to do. They may also note that Steve has to decide what is meant by 'come close' to the bush. It may be too that the insects are visiting the open flowers.

b Results will depend on the kinds of balls used in the experiments and the number of trials. The height from which the balls are dropped will also affect results.

c The important information to be gleaned from the map is that the rainfall is more acid in North-eastern England and the eastern side generally.

WATCHPOINTS

● Remind the children that the balls are to be dropped, not bounced.

● The material on the Extend sheet source: *Key Data*, 1990. Crown Copyright 1990. Reproduced by permission of the Controller of HMSO and of the Office for National Statistics.

Assessment of learning outcomes

a Responses to questioning on the Help sheet data.

b Conduct of the experiment and results table on the Workbook page.

c Observations made on the Extend sheet.

Line graphs

Learning intentions

a Know how to draw a line graph.

b Create a line graph.

c Interpret a line graph.

Vocabulary

Axis, axes, graph, line graph, plot, scale, X, Y

Lesson pattern

Whole class, practical work in pairs and Workbook page, Extend sheet

RESOURCES AND SETTING UP

a The introduction and activity **a** could be done on a previous day, or in a maths session.

b Workbook page. For each pair of children the following are required: thermometer suitable for reading accurately temperatures on the 20–90° C range beaker of warm water. Try the experiment out before the lesson. Air temperature will affect the rate of cooling. It may be wise to have the water quite hot to start with, depending on classroom temperatures.

c Extend sheet.

ACTIVITIES

INTRODUCTION

● In a maths session, or in groups, before the lesson, go into activity **a**.

a Show the children how to draw a line graph. Tell them what a graph is and why we draw them. Check that they understand the power of data presented in this way. Give the children the chance to draw a graph using secondary data, during a maths session.

b In pairs allow the children to record the temperature of water as it cools over time, and draw a graph of their results on the Workbook page.

c The children are required to inspect and interpret the line graph on the Extend sheet.

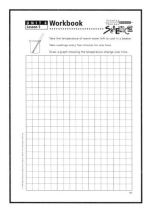

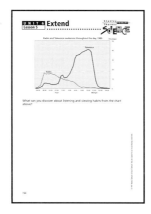

OUTCOMES

EXPECTED RESULTS

 The children should understand that a graph is a diagrammatic way of presenting information. A line graph looks at the relationship between two sets of information – that is how one changes with the other. One set of information arranged vertically up the page is set on the 'Y' axis. The other arranged horizontally goes along the 'X' axis.

b Using an appropriate scale the children should be able to chart the fall in temperature of the water. The resulting graph should start higher on the 'Y' axis and then drop away.

c There are a number of intriguing comments that can be made by looking at the data on the graph. For example, radio listening peaks in the morning, TV in the evening. Many more people watch TV than listen to the radio.

WATCHPOINTS

● The experimental demands mean this lesson probably requires more than the allotted hour.

⚠ Warn the children of the dangers of very hot water. (Any temperature above about 55°C will be too hot to touch.) Make sure the containers used are stable and will not easily be knocked over.

● Check that the thermometer temperature ranges are appropriate for the temperatures to be measured. If the children need reminding, show them how to read a thermometer accurately.

● The chart of 'Radio and television audiences throughout the day, 1989, United Kingdom' comes from *Social Trends, 1990, Chart 10.5*, Key Data 90, © Crown copyright, 1990.

Assessment of learning outcomes

 Judgements should be made of line graphs each child has attempted.

 Workbook page.

 Extend sheet.

Data patterns

Learning intentions

a Identify data patterns.

b Collate data sets revealing patterns.

c Identify data sets that may yield patterns.

Vocabulary

Bar chart, conclusions, data patterns, interpret

Lesson pattern

Whole class, work group and Help sheet, whole class, pairs or work groups and Workbook page, Extend sheet

RESOURCES AND SETTING UP

a Help sheet.

b Workbook page. Dinner registers for classes in the school (sufficient for the children to have at least one for each work group). If there are few classes, photocopy parts of some registers before the lesson.
Identify three sample weeks in the school year when it is anticipated that there would be interesting data patterns (e.g. Christmas lunch). Squared and plain paper is needed for data presentation.

c Extend sheet. Squared and plain paper may be required.

ACTIVITIES

INTRODUCTION

● Remind the children about the presentation of information in a bar chart.

a Allow the children in their work groups, to look at copies of the Help sheet and discuss the bar charts they see there. After a few minutes call the children together to give their comments to the whole class group.

b Ask the children to investigate the sample weeks on the dinner register and record their findings on the Workbook page. (See note under Watchpoints.)

c The extension activity offers children the chance to locate other weeks of the year where significant data patterns may emerge.

OUTCOMES

EXPECTED RESULTS

 In the feedback discussion the children may light on some of the following ideas.

- There are no really outstanding patterns in the data presented.
- No girls are born in May and July where there are five boys' birthdays.
- If the class is a 'school year class', the girls in the class are older than the boys on average because most of their birthdays fall between September and March.

....

b Having drawn bar charts showing numbers having dinners and packed lunches the children should be able to find data patterns.

....

c The outcomes here will depend on the pattern of take up of school meals/packed lunches in the weeks the children choose.

WATCHPOINTS

- The children may need advice about assembling the rough data before trying to draw a bar chart. If the numbers of children entered on the dinner registers are small the children may be able to do a boy/girl breakdown of the figures.

- If dinner registers are unavailable, or if their use would be inappropriate, attendance registers may yield interesting patterns.

Assessment of learning outcomes

a Initial discussion and contribution to the class.

....

b Work on activity **b** and interpretations of bar charts.

....

c Extend sheet.

Identifying what is important

Learning intentions

a Identify key factors in experiments.

b Carry through an experiment noting key factors.

c Devise an experiment isolating key factors.

Vocabulary

'Control', factors, variables

Lesson pattern

Whole class or workgroup and Help sheet, practical work and Workbook page, Extend sheet

---

RESOURCES AND SETTING UP

a Help sheet.

b Workbook page. Magnifiers giving different strengths of magnification, three for each group attempting this experiment. The magnifiers should, ideally, all be the same size. If they are marked with the magnification achieved mask this information for this lesson. Measuring tapes and metre sticks are needed.

c Extend sheet. Three different cycling helmets. These are not essential but would be useful for display purposes and to stimulate the children's ideas.

ACTIVITIES

INTRODUCTION

● Make it clear to the children that it is very important to the success of work in science, that it is properly planned. Before beginning to try to find things out, scientists think very carefully about what might happen, how measurements should be taken, what observations and measures to take, what might 'go wrong'. This kind of thinking is required in this lesson. Either conduct a discussion of the issues on the Help sheet in a whole class, or allow the children to do so first in their work groups.

a The children should inspect the experiments planned on the Help sheet and try to work out some of the important issues for the experimenters.

b Working in pairs or work groups ask half the class to try Clive's experiment and the other half to try James' experiment from the Help sheet. The work can be written up on the Workbook page.

c This presents the children with a novel experimental setting where they are again required to think hard about which the important issues are.

OUTCOMES

EXPECTED RESULTS

a Here are some of the key factors the children may suggest.

Clive's experiment How will Clive measure the magnifying power? Does the distance between the magnifier and the object matter? Does the distance between the eye and the magnifier matter? What is Clive going to magnify? Should it be the same thing each time?

Kara's experiment What does it say on the baking powder pack? Should Kara try these

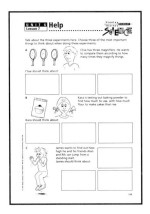

recommendations? Should other ingredients like sugar be varied along with flour and baking powder? Can measuring be done with spoons or scales? How can the amount the cakes have risen be measured?

James' experiment Should the boys stand with their feet together? Can the boys bend their knees before leaving the ground? How can the height of the jump be measured? What is the 'height of the jump'? Is it distance of feet from the floor? Does the boys' overall height or weight affect their jump?

b Results here will depend on exactly how the children decide to carry through the experiments. They should reveal additional important issues that could be considered in planning the experiment.

c The results will depend on the ideas the children have. Here are some experimental ideas:

- How well do they fit the human head?
- Do the helmets adjust to fit different shapes of human head?
- Can the helmets be seen in poor light conditions/the dark?
- Are the strap fixings secure?
- Is there any stretch on the straps.

WATCHPOINTS

- Children should not hit or apply force to actual cycle helmets as this could cause a weakness in the helmet.

Assessment of learning outcomes

a Contributions to discussion and entries on the Help sheet.

b Conduct and involvement in the experiment and record on the Workbook page.

c Ideas offered on the Extend sheet.

Choosing and using apparatus

Learning intentions

a Identify measures to be made in an experiment.

b Choose appropriate apparatus for an experiment.

c Improve on choices of experimental apparatus.

Vocabulary

Apparatus, 'degree of accuracy', measures

Lesson pattern

Whole class, practical work in pairs and Workbook page, Extend sheet

RESOURCES AND SETTING UP

a **b** Workbook page. Before the lesson use several copies of the the Help sheet. Cut them up so that each investigation is on a separate strip of paper. Stick them onto thin card. Each pair of children will require one of these. The children will require access to a whole array of apparatus. Set out somewhere in the room a mix of apparatus including at least the following: measuring cylinders, beakers, washing bowls, teapots and mugs, Newton meters, string, clamps and clamp stands, thermometers, timers, aquaria, cocktail sticks, blindfold.

c Extend sheet.

ACTIVITIES

INTRODUCTION

● Remind the children of the work they have done in previous years and this year where the choice of apparatus has been crucial. Check that they understand that scientists choose the pieces of apparatus that are appropriate for the experiments they are doing and that this includes measuring tools. Measuring tools vary according to how accurate the measurements taken with them are. When scientists talk about 'degrees of accuracy' they are referring to the sensitivity of the tool and the scientist to the measures required.

a The children should listen to the introduction and instructions for activity **b**.

b In pairs the children should pick 'out of a hat' one of the card strips with an investigation on it. They are then required to work out what they would do in this experiment and what apparatus they would require. They should then fetch that apparatus from the array set out, put it all together and display their investigation title in front of it. Their work can be recorded on the Workbook page. Then they can inspect the arrays of apparatus set out by other pairs in response to the challenges. The children can exchange suggestions. Finish this part of the session with a class discussion of choices made.

c Using the Extend sheet the children should make choices about apparatus used in a range of settings.

OUTCOMES

EXPECTED RESULTS

a The children now have considerable experience of choosing and using apparatus and should now know of the importance of 'fitness for purpose'.

b The apparatus chosen and listed by the children will vary according to how they propose their investigation should be conducted.

c Here are some suggested answers (the children may be able to justify the choice of other pieces of apparatus):

– Elijah may have used a pipette or dropper.
– Gus needs kitchen scales.
– Paula could have used a deeper container (though cooking oil is viscous it may well spill).
– Geena would find it difficult to get a reading in the air in the room and a clinical thermometer measures only the range possible in live human beings. An ordinary thermometer would be better for the job.
– Lee cannot use a plane mirror to magnify. A magnifier is a lens.
– Neil will take a long time to measure a running track with such a small ruler. A click wheel or surveyor's tape would be better.

– Sandy needs a dropper or at least a much smaller container from which to get one drop. Kim can join wires with string, but a good contact is essential and crocodile clips may be better.

WATCHPOINTS

● The children may wish to take copies of the Help sheet home to do some further thinking.

Assessment of learning outcomes

a Attention to the introduction.

b Paired work and the Workbook page.

c Extend sheet.

Repeating an experiment

Learning intentions

a Know why experiments are repeated.

b Repeat an experiment.

c Collate results of repeated experiments.

Vocabulary

Average, repetition, replicate, trial

Lesson pattern

Whole class, practical work in pairs and Workbook page, Extend sheet

RESOURCES AND SETTING UP

b Workbook page. Each work group needs: card pieces from which the children can cut and fold marble runs as shown on the Workbook page, marbles of different sizes, small wooden blocks, measuring tapes and metre sticks, a space large enough for all the children to allow the marbles to run down the ramp and come to rest.

c Extend sheet.

ACTIVITIES

INTRODUCTION

● Ask the children why they think experiments are repeated and what they understand by 'trialling'.

a The children should listen in and contribute to the introduction.

b The children should, working in pairs, work groups, or alone if the teacher wishes, carry through one of the two investigations set out on the Workbook page. They either need one marble and a block they move under the run, or two marbles and a block that is left in position under the run.

c The children can comment on their experiment done in **b** above, on the Extend sheet, and repeat the experiment with the marble, this time over ten trials.

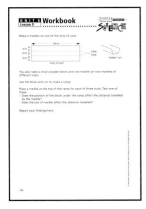

OUTCOMES

EXPECTED RESULTS

a The children should know that these are some of the reasons that experiments are repeated:

- to check that results were accurately measured the first time.
- to see how wide the range of possible results is.
- to gather data for working out averages.
- to check that the whole experiment can be replicated.

b Results will vary according to the size of block, tilt of ramp and mass of marble.

c Ten trials should yield a more accurate judgement (than three trials) of the average distance travelled and the likely range of results in the prevailing conditions.

WATCHPOINTS

 Remind the children that the marble should be set down at the top of the ramp, and not given a push.

Assessment of learning outcomes

a Attention to the introduction.

b Conduct of the investigation and the Workbook page.

c Extend sheet.

Coming to conclusions

Learning intentions

a Know what a 'conclusion' is.

b Draw conclusions.

c Know how conclusions can be modified.

Vocabulary

Conclusion, findings, results

Lesson pattern

Whole class, practical work and Workbook page, practical work and Extend sheet

RESOURCES AND SETTING UP

b Workbook page. Before the lesson collect fingerprints from a number of people. They could be children in the class or members of staff or of the family. Give the owners of the fingerprints imaginary names. Display the fingerprints, along with those of the 'culprit' of some misdemeanour. Arrange in a workshop setting that the children can examine all the fingerprints and those of the culprit. Magnifiers (ideally one each for the whole class; if this is not possible one between two).

c Extend sheet. Enough of the following for those pairs of children who finish activity **b** (it may be the whole class in this lesson):

chocolate beans, blotting paper, scissors, beakers of water, sticky tape.

ACTIVITIES

INTRODUCTION

● Ask the children what they understand by the word 'conclusion'. Conclusions are judgements and decisions reached on the basis of evidence. (Scientists should not 'jump to conclusions'.)

a The children should attend to the introduction.

b In pairs (or alone if there are enough magnifiers) allow the children to go around the room and carefully examine all the sample fingerprints. They should then reach their own conclusions and explain how they have done so. Their work can be recorded on the Workbook page.

c Using the Extend sheet the children can set up the chocolate bean experiment, examine the evidence, and again draw conclusions. The children can make a record of what they have done on the Extend sheet.

OUTCOMES

EXPECTED RESULTS

a The children should be able to make the meaning of conclusion explicit.

b Having gone through the process of examining evidence and drawing conclusions, the children should have a good understanding of what 'drawing conclusions' means.

c The children should carry through the experiment and demonstrate that they can draw conclusions. Beyond that, they can predict what causes scientists to modify conclusions. In trials dark brown and mauve sugar coated chocolate beans yielded more than one dye colour.

WATCHPOINTS

● If an overhead projector is available the fingerprints could be enlarged (after the lesson) so that the children can see the details of the prints.

Assessment of learning outcomes

a Attention to the introduction.

b Conduct of the workshop and the Workbook page.

c Conduct of the experiment and Extend sheet.

Famous scientists

Learning intentions

a Know of the importance of the work of some scientists.

b Find out about the life and work of a famous scientist.

c Complete a scientific apparatus quiz.

Vocabulary

Names of the scientists on the Workbook page

Lesson pattern

Group or individual work,
Workbook page and Help sheet,
Extend sheet

RESOURCES AND SETTING UP

a **b** Help sheet. Books, CD-ROMs and other sources (e.g. from local and national museums) about famous scientists. All the children need access to these sources, so if they are in short supply, some pages of information need to be copied prior to the lesson.

c Extend sheet. Children will need scissors and card and Plasticine or other modelling material.

ACTIVITIES

INTRODUCTION

● The children can go straight into the activities.

a **b** In work groups or alone the children should inspect the list of scientists on the Workbook page and find out all they can about one of them. The information they collect can be put into the little book that can be made up from the Help sheet.

c Ask the children to see if they can identify the apparatus displayed on the Extend sheet.

OUTCOMES

EXPECTED RESULTS

a **b** The children should retrieve and assemble information about at least one famous scientist.

c The answers are as follows:

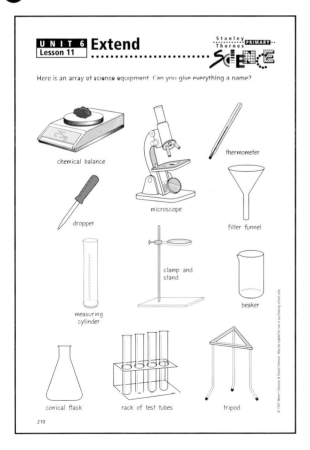

WATCHPOINTS

● If there are local connections with famous scientists, these can be explored through the local museum or history society.

Assessment of learning outcomes

a **b** Information retrieval and booklet created out of the Help sheet.

c Numbers of correct answers on the Extend sheet.

Review

- Adjust seating arrangements to test conditions.

a **b** Workbook pages 1 and 2.

c Extend sheet.

ACTIVITIES

Ask the children to complete the Workbook pages. Those who finish can make up the scientific toy on the Extend sheet.

WATCHPOINTS

- The scientific toy is intended as an introduction to ideas about balance and centre of gravity which will feature in Year 6/P7 of the course.

- Remind the children that they can also complete their own checklist about the unit when they have time. The checklist can be found at the end of the material for this unit in the photocopiable resources.

OUTCOMES

EXPECTED ANSWERS

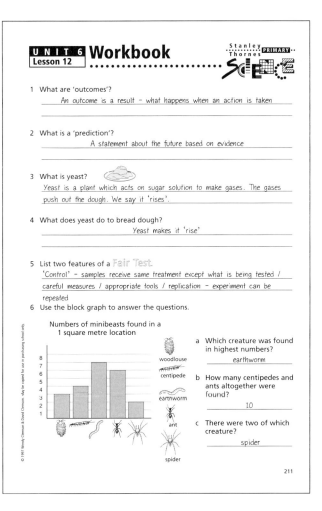

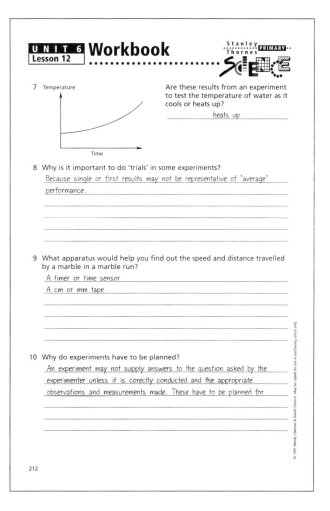

Links between Year 5 Stanley Thornes Primary Science and the National Curriculum Programmes of Study

UNIT 1: SOLIDS, LIQUIDS AND GASES

GENERAL PROGRAMME OF STUDY

EXPERIMENTAL AND INVESTIGATIVE SCIENCE

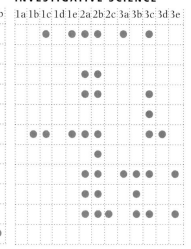

UNIT 2: BODY WORKS

GENERAL PROGRAMME OF STUDY

EXPERIMENTAL AND INVESTIGATIVE SCIENCE

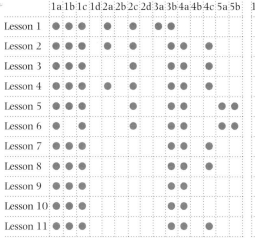
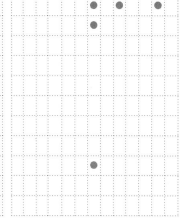

UNIT 3: IMPORTANT FORCES

GENERAL PROGRAMME OF STUDY

EXPERIMENTAL AND INVESTIGATIVE SCIENCE

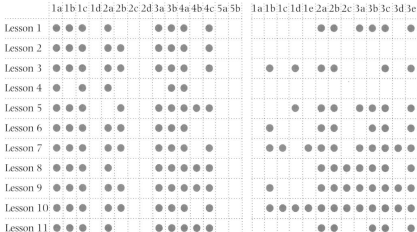

MATERIALS AND THEIR PROPERTIES

PHYSICAL PROCESSES

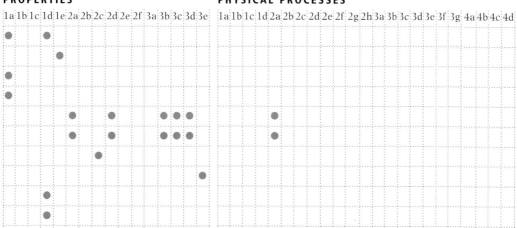

1a 1b 1c 1d 1e 2a 2b 2c 2d 2e 2f 3a 3b 3c 3d 3e   1a 1b 1c 1d 2a 2b 2c 2d 2e 2f 2g 2h 3a 3b 3c 3d 3e 3f 3g 4a 4b 4c 4d

LIFE PROCESSES AND LIVING THINGS

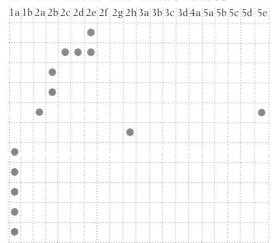

1a 1b 2a 2b 2c 2d 2e 2f 2g 2h 3a 3b 3c 3d 4a 5a 5b 5c 5d 5e

PHYSICAL PROCESSES

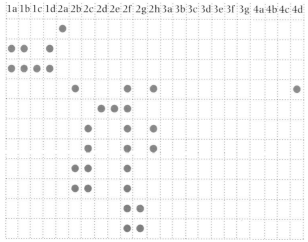

1a 1b 1c 1d 2a 2b 2c 2d 2e 2f 2g 2h 3a 3b 3c 3d 3e 3f 3g 4a 4b 4c 4d

UNIT 4: LIVING THINGS IN THEIR ENVIRONMENT

GENERAL PROGRAMME OF STUDY

	1a	1b	1c	1d	2a	2b	2c	2d	3a	3b	4a	4b	4c	5a	5b
Lesson 1	●	●	●					●		●					
Lesson 2	●	●	●					●		●	●				
Lesson 3	●	●	●					●		●					
Lesson 4	●	●	●					●		●	●				
Lesson 5	●	●		●				●	●	●	●				
Lesson 6	●	●	●	●				●	●	●	●		●		
Lesson 7	●	●	●			●	●	●		●				●	●
Lesson 8	●	●	●		●		●	●	●	●	●				
Lesson 9	●		●					●	●		●				
Lesson 10	●		●					●	●		●				
Lesson 11	●		●				●	●	●		●				

EXPERIMENTAL AND INVESTIGATIVE SCIENCE

	1a	1b	1c	1d	1e	2a	2b	2c	3a	3b	3c	3d	3e
Lesson 1													
Lesson 2							●						
Lesson 3							●						
Lesson 4							●						
Lesson 5												●	
Lesson 6												●	
Lesson 7													
Lesson 8										●		●	

UNIT 5: SOUND, LIGHT AND THE SOLAR SYSTEM

GENERAL PROGRAMME OF STUDY

	1a	1b	1c	1d	2a	2b	2c	2d	3a	3b	4a	4b	4c	5a	5b
Lesson 1	●	●	●		●	●			●	●	●				
Lesson 2	●	●	●			●			●	●		●			
Lesson 3	●	●	●			●			●	●		●	●		
Lesson 4	●														
Lesson 5	●	●	●		●	●			●	●	●				
Lesson 6	●	●	●			●			●	●		●			
Lesson 7	●	●	●			●			●	●					
Lesson 8	●		●			●			●	●					
Lesson 9	●		●			●			●	●					
Lesson 10	●		●			●			●	●					
Lesson 11	●		●			●			●	●					

EXPERIMENTAL AND INVESTIGATIVE SCIENCE

	1a	1b	1c	1d	1e	2a	2b	2c	3a	3b	3c	3d	3e
Lesson 1						●	●				●		●
Lesson 2						●	●		●	●	●		
Lesson 3						●	●						
Lesson 4													
Lesson 5						●	●			●			
Lesson 6							●	●					
Lesson 7							●				●		

UNIT 6: BEING A SCIENTIST

GENERAL PROGRAMME OF STUDY

	1a	1b	1c	1d	2a	2b	2c	2d	3a	3b	4a	4b	4c	5a	5b
Lesson 1	●	●	●					●	●	●					
Lesson 2	●	●	●	●				●	●	●					
Lesson 3	●	●	●	●				●	●	●					
Lesson 4	●	●	●	●			●	●	●	●					
Lesson 5	●	●	●	●				●	●	●					
Lesson 6	●	●	●				●		●						
Lesson 7	●	●	●			●	●	●	●	●					
Lesson 8	●							●	●						
Lesson 9	●	●	●		●		●	●	●	●					
Lesson 10	●	●	●		●										
Lesson 11	●														

EXPERIMENTAL AND INVESTIGATIVE SCIENCE

	1a	1b	1c	1d	1e	2a	2b	2c	3a	3b	3c	3d	3e
Lesson 1	●	●	●	●	●	●	●			●	●	●	●
Lesson 2							●			●		●	●
Lesson 3	●	●	●	●	●	●	●			●	●	●	●
Lesson 4		●	●			●	●	●	●	●	●	●	
Lesson 5			●			●	●	●	●		●	●	
Lesson 6						●	●		●	●			
Lesson 7	●	●				●	●	●	●	●	●	●	
Lesson 8						●							
Lesson 9							●	●	●	●	●		●
Lesson 10							●						

LIFE PROCESSES AND LIVING THINGS

	1a	1b	2a	2b	2c	2d	2e	2f	2g	2h	3a	3b	3c	3d	4a
Lesson 1														●	

LIFE PROCESSES AND LIVING THINGS

1a 1b 2a 2b 2c 2d 2e 2f 2g 2h 3a 3b 3c 3d 4a 5a 5b 5c 5d 5e

MATERIALS AND THEIR PROPERTIES

1a 1b 1c 1d 1e 2a 2b 2c 2d 2e 2f 3a 3b 3c 3d 3e

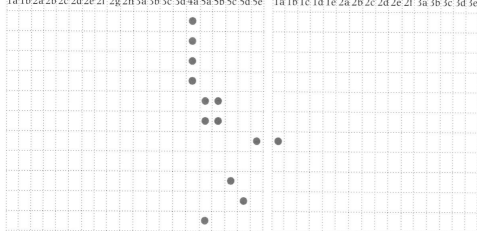

MATERIALS AND THEIR PROPERTIES

1a 1b 1c 1d 1e 2a 2b 2c 2d 2e 2f 3a 3b 3c 3d 3e

PHYSICAL PROCESSES

1a 1b 1c 1d 2a 2b 2c 2d 2e 2f 2g 2h 3a 3b 3c 3d 3e 3f 3g 4a 4b 4c 4d

MATERIALS AND THEIR PROPERTIES

5a 5b 5c 5d 5e 1a 1b 1c 1d 1e 2a 2b 2c 2d 2e 2f 3a 3b 3c 3d 3e

PHYSICAL PROCESSES

1a 1b 1c 1d 2a 2b 2c 2d 2e 2f 2g 2h 3a 3b 3c 3d 3e 3f 3g 4a 4b 4c 4d

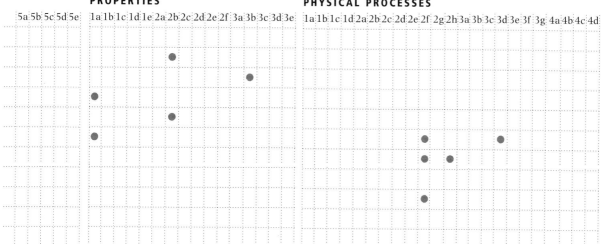

Links between Year 5/P6 Stanley Thornes Primary Science and Environmental Studies 5–14

Attainment outcomes: key features
Stages P4 to P6

Understanding Living Things and the Processes of Life

Variety and characteristic features

• the main distinguishing features of vertebrates, major invertebrate groups, flowering and non-flowering plants;	Unit 2 / Lesson 7, 8, 10, 11 Unit 4 / Lessons 1, 3, 5, 6
• recognising and naming some members of these groups using simple keys;	Unit 4 / Lessons 2, 4
• similarities and differences between plants and animals of the same species.	Unit 4 / Lesson 1

The processes of life

• the structure and functions of the major parts of the body as they relate to the processes of movement and nutrition;	Unit 2 / Lessons 4, 9
• the structure and functions of the parts of flowering plants and factors which affect germination and growth;	
• dispersal of fruits and seeds by animals, by wind and by self.	

Interaction of living things with their environment

• the interaction between humans and their environment in relation to aspects such as farming, fishing and other local industries;	
• simple food chains based on energy from the sun;	Unit 4 / Lesson 10
• the importance of conservation and of the value of re-cycling materials;	Unit 4 / Lesson 11
• living things which are very rare or which have become extinct.	
• how plants and animals are affected by environmental conditions.	

Understanding Energy and Forces

Forms and sources of energy

• the Sun as the main source of light and heat;	
• sound from a variety of vibrating sources;	Unit 5 / Lesson 2
• electricity as a form of energy;	Unit 3 / Lessons 2, 3
• sources of electrical energy.	Unit 3 / Lessons 2, 3

Properties and uses of energy

• use of thermometers to measure 'hotness', leading to distinction between heat and temperature;	Unit 6 / Lesson 5
• sunlight and shadows;	Unit 5 / Lessons 3, 4
• mirrors and reflections, including curved mirrors;	Unit 5 / Lesson 5
• lenses;	
• colours in sunlight, visible spectrum formed by a prism;	
• simple applications of mirrors and lenses;	
• pitch and volume of sounds including applications;	Unit 5 / Lesson 2
• electrical conductors and insulators;	
• construction of battery operated circuits to operate;	Unit 3 / Lessons 2, 3
• electrical safety.	

Conversion and transfer of energy

• simple introduction to the idea that one form of energy can be converted to another.	

Forces and their effects

• friction forces on different surfaces, reducing friction;	Unit 3 / Lessons 2, 6, 7
• air resistance, streamlining;	Unit 3 / Lessons 8, 9
• force of gravity;	Unit 3 / Lesson 4
• magnetic materials, forces of attraction and repulsion;	Unit 3 / Lesson 1
• motion down a slope under gravity;	Unit 6 / Lesson 9
• Earth's magnetic field and the compass;	Unit 3 / Lesson 1
• magnetic materials in everyday use.	

Understanding Earth and Space

Earth in space

- the planets of the solar system;

  Unit 5 / Lesson 9

- measuring the passage of time.

  Unt 5 / Lesson 10

On planet Earth

- the Earth's atmosphere;

- the water cycle (in simple outline) introducing water as a gas, melting, freezing, evaporation, condensation;

  Unit 1 / Lesson 5

- patterns of weather observed locally.

Materials from Earth

- uses of water, methods of water conservation;

- further properties of common materials;

  Unit 1 / Lesson 1   Unit 4 / Lesson 7
  Unit 5 / Lesson 1   Unit 6 / Lessons 4, 6

- natural and manufactured materials and simple examples of re-cyling;

- how materials can be changed.

  Unit 1 / Lessons 5–7 Unit 6 / Lesson 2, 5

Record keeping sheet

Year 5/P6
Child's name _____ Class/Year _____ Teacher's initials _____

Tick activities successfully completed.

	Unit 1			Unit 2		
Lesson 1	a	b	c	a	b	c
Lesson 2	a	b	c	a	b	c
Lesson 3	a	b	c	a	b	c
Lesson 4	a	b	c	a	b	c
Lesson 5	a	b	c	a	b	c
Lesson 6	a	b	c	a	b	c
Lesson 7	a	b	c	a	b	c
Lesson 8	a	b	c	a	b	c
Lesson 9	a	b	c	a	b	c
Lesson 10	a	b	c	a	b	c
Lesson 11	a	b	c	a	b	c
Lesson 12	ab		c	ab		c

	Unit 3			Unit 4		
Lesson 1	a	b	c	a	b	c
Lesson 2	a	b	c	a	b	c
Lesson 3	a	b	c	a	b	c
Lesson 4	a	b	c	a	b	c
Lesson 5	a	b	c	a	b	c
Lesson 6	a	b	c	a	b	c
Lesson 7	a	b	c	a	b	c
Lesson 8	a	b	c	a	b	c
Lesson 9	a	b	c	a	b	c
Lesson 10	a	b	c	a	b	c
Lesson 11	a	b	c	a	b	c
Lesson 12	ab		c	ab		c

	Unit 5			Unit 6		
Lesson 1	a	b	c	a	b	c
Lesson 2	a	b	c	a	b	c
Lesson 3	a	b	c	a	b	c
Lesson 4	a	b	c	a	b	c
Lesson 5	a	b	c	a	b	c
Lesson 6	a	b	c	a	b	c
Lesson 7	a	b	c	a	b	c
Lesson 8	a	b	c	a	b	c
Lesson 9	a	b	c	a	b	c
Lesson 10	a	b	c	a	b	c
Lesson 11	a	b	c	a	b	c
Lesson 12	ab		c	ab		c

National Curriculum of England and Wales
Mostly 'a's = Working towards Level 4
Mostly 'a's and 'b's = Level 4
'a's, 'b's and 'c's = Working towards Level 5 or beyond
Environmental Studies 5–14, Scotland
Mostly 'a's = Working towards Level C
Mostly 'a's and 'b's = Level C
'a's, 'b's and 'c's = Working towards Level D or beyond

Equipment list

The following science equipment is required for Year 5/P6 of this course:

Bar magnets
Iron filings
Slings to support swinging magnets
Batteries
Circuit wire and wire cutters
Crocodile clips
Bulb holders
Lamp bulbs
Switches
Bells
Buzzers

Camera and film
Accurate classroom balances
Measuring jugs or cubes
Minute timers, watches or clock with minute hands
A clock with an audible tick
30 cm rulers
Metre measuring sticks
Measuring tapes
Measuring tapes for long distances
Trundle wheels
Weighing masses
Newton meters
Hydrometer

Litmus paper
Universal indicator

Forehead thermometer
Celsius thermometers

Transparent tanks, aquaria or vivaria
Beakers
Droppers
Clamps and stands
Funnels
Rigid plastic sheets (or similar washable surface for friction experiments)

Magnifiers
Plane safety mirrors
Light box with slit filter and colour filters
A room with blackout facilities
A screen
Overhead projector
Pocket torches

Tuning fork

Wooden blocks
A globe
Plasticine
Clay
Plaster of Paris
Soil, rock and mineral samples
Soil test kits
Wire
Cup hooks

Newton meter

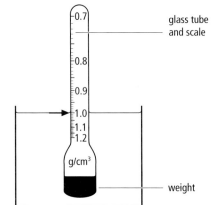

hydrometer

glass tube and scale

weight

Light box – light boxes vary. This diagram shows the principles behind its working.

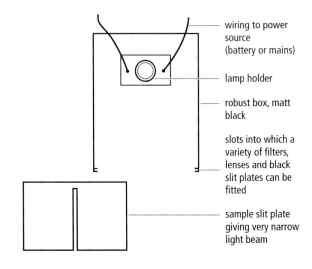

wiring to power source (battery or mains)

lamp holder

robust box, matt black

slots into which a variety of filters, lenses and black slit plates can be fitted

sample slit plate giving very narrow light beam